"*Bringing the Word to Life: Scripture Messages that Change Lives*
focuses on scripture readings for all Sunday and Solemnity
Masses. Author Michael R. Kent, a psychologist dedicated to
spiritual as well as mental healing, talks about the day's scripture
as common textual ground between himself and the reader and
suggests how it can inform our lives and promote spiritual well-
being."

Paul Matthew St. Pierre
The British Columbia Catholic

"Kent has examined the readings for each Sunday and feast 'to
glean one specific insight that, if acknowledged and put into
practice, could be instrumental in improving the quality of one's
life...' He reminds us to simplify our lifestyle, to slow down our
hyperactivity, to take time to smell the roses, to forgive, and to be
kind to the members of our family and neighborhood. These
messages can be useful to anyone searching for 'an enhanced
quality of life.'"

The Prairie Messenger

"Kent really has an awareness of people's emotions and thoughts
as he directs his comments to the readings and makes sense out
of them. He gets to the heart of the matter in each of his essays
and offers ample opportunity for reflection and spiritual growth.
"These reflections are offered to anyone searching for an
enhanced quality of life and willing to use the inexhaustible riches of the Word of God as a resource for a deeper spirituality. This
book can be used as a resource for preachers, Bible study groups,
classroom teachers, and parish personnel. It also includes a helpful index that sorts the readings by topics and themes."

Peggy Weber
Catholic Observer

"I find *Bringing the Word to Life* an intriguing departure from the usual commentary on Scripture. The book identifies a single message that ties together the Sunday readings, applies the message to daily life through examples to which people in the pews will resonate, then gives specific insights for effective living based on the message. An admirable way for both homilists and study groups to guarantee that 'My word shall not return to me empty.'"

Rev. Msgr. Francis P. Friedl
Co-author, *Homilies Alive:*
Creating Homilies that Hit Home

"Michael Kent's *Bringing the Word to Life* is rich food for growth in Christian living. The reflections are contemporary and direct. The meditations offer fresh insights into the perennial Good News of Jesus Christ. The questions after each reflection lead to a deepening understanding of God and self. Thus, this book is an effective support for individual development, a stimulating catalyst for group discussion, and a meaty resource for homily preparation."

Sydney Condray
Author, *Assembled in Christ*

YEAR C

Bringing the WORD *to Life*

Scripture Messages
That Change Lives

MICHAEL R. KENT

TWENTY-THIRD PUBLICATIONS
Mystic, CT 06355

Twenty-Third Publications
185 Willow Street
P.O. Box 180
Mystic, CT 06355
(860) 536-2611
800-321-0411

ISBN 0-89622-731-6
Library of Congress Catalog Card Number 94-61926
Printed in the U.S.A.

CONTENTS

INTRODUCTION   1

FIRST SUNDAY OF ADVENT
Living Righteously   3

SECOND SUNDAY OF ADVENT
Digging at the Roots   5

THIRD SUNDAY OF ADVENT
Joy in the Ordinary   7

FOURTH SUNDAY OF ADVENT
Trust the Grand Design   9

CHRISTMAS
Birth of Possibilities   11

HOLY FAMILY
Seat of Learning   13

SOLEMNITY OF MARY, MOTHER OF GOD
(NEW YEAR'S DAY)
Hospitality   15

EPIPHANY
Child of Great Promise   17

BAPTISM OF THE LORD
Developing Resources   19

ASH WEDNESDAY
Now Is the Acceptable Time   21

FIRST SUNDAY OF LENT
Personal Allegiance to Jesus   23

SECOND SUNDAY OF LENT
Able to See   25

THIRD SUNDAY OF LENT
Second Chance   27

FOURTH SUNDAY OF LENT
Grace of Forgiveness   29

FIFTH SUNDAY OF LENT
But for the Grace of God   31

PASSION (PALM) SUNDAY
The Name of Jesus   33

HOLY THURSDAY
Gathering of Friends   35

GOOD FRIDAY
Overcome Evil with Good   37

EASTER
Light at the End of the Tunnel   39

SECOND SUNDAY OF EASTER
Faith People   41

THIRD SUNDAY OF EASTER
Try Something Different   43

FOURTH SUNDAY OF EASTER
Adult Christianity   45

FIFTH SUNDAY OF EASTER
Love Is What Love Does   47

SIXTH SUNDAY OF EASTER
Take Advantage of the Spirit   49

ASCENSION
Accept Affirmation 51

SEVENTH SUNDAY OF EASTER
Stay Connected 53

PENTECOST
Living with Passion 55

SOLEMNITY OF THE HOLY TRINITY
The Wonder of God 57

SECOND SUNDAY IN ORDINARY TIME
Live From Your Strengths 59

THIRD SUNDAY IN ORDINARY TIME
We Are One 61

FOURTH SUNDAY IN ORDINARY TIME
Test of Adulthood 63

FIFTH SUNDAY IN ORDINARY TIME
Leave It Behind 65

SIXTH SUNDAY IN ORDINARY TIME
Blessings in Disguise 67

SEVENTH SUNDAY IN ORDINARY TIME
The Heart Has Its Reasons 69

EIGHTH SUNDAY IN ORDINARY TIME
If the Shoe Fits 71

NINTH SUNDAY IN ORDINARY TIME
Broaden Your Horizons 73

TENTH SUNDAY IN ORDINARY TIME
   Death Brings Appreciation of Life   75

THE BODY AND BLOOD OF CHRIST (CORPUS CHRISTI)
   Nothing Neutral   77

ELEVENTH SUNDAY IN ORDINARY TIME
   Love and the Law   79

TWELFTH SUNDAY IN ORDINARY TIME
   Lose Your Life   81

THIRTEENTH SUNDAY IN ORDINARY TIME
   No Excuses   83

FOURTEENTH SUNDAY IN ORDINARY TIME
   A New Creation   85

FIFTEENTH SUNDAY IN ORDINARY TIME
   Who Is My Neighbor?   87

SIXTEENTH SUNDAY IN ORDINARY TIME
   A Matter of Priorities   89

SEVENTEENTH SUNDAY IN ORDINARY TIME
   Seek and Find   91

EIGHTEENTH SUNDAY IN ORDINARY TIME
   Vanity of Vanities   93

NINETEENTH SUNDAY IN ORDINARY TIME
   Fear Not   95

ASSUMPTION OF THE VIRGIN MARY
   Channel of Grace   97

TWENTIETH SUNDAY IN ORDINARY TIME
Comfortable Religion 99

TWENTY-FIRST SUNDAY IN ORDINARY TIME
Discipline 101

TWENTY-SECOND SUNDAY IN ORDINARY TIME
Humility 103

TWENTY-THIRD SUNDAY IN ORDINARY TIME
Detachment 105

TWENTY-FOURTH SUNDAY IN ORDINARY TIME
When They're Ready 107

TWENTY-FIFTH SUNDAY IN ORDINARY TIME
Little Things Count 109

TWENTY-SIXTH SUNDAY IN ORDINARY TIME
Willpower 111

TWENTY-SEVENTH SUNDAY IN ORDINARY TIME
Empower Yourself 113

TWENTY-EIGHTH SUNDAY IN ORDINARY TIME
Where Are the Other Nine? 115

TWENTY-NINTH SUNDAY IN ORDINARY TIME
As Long As It Takes 117

THIRTIETH SUNDAY IN ORDINARY TIME
Does Prayer Work? 119

ALL SAINTS
Pure of Heart 121

ALL THE FAITHFUL DEPARTED (ALL SOULS)
Death's Gift of Meaning 123

THIRTY-FIRST SUNDAY IN ORDINARY TIME
Welcome the Outcast 125

THIRTY-SECOND SUNDAY IN ORDINARY TIME
God of the Living 127

THIRTY-THIRD SUNDAY IN ORDINARY TIME
Faithfulness 129

THANKSGIVING
Pay Attention 131

CHRIST THE KING
(THIRTY-FOURTH SUNDAY IN ORDINARY TIME)
Shift at Center 133

TOPICS AND THEMES 135

SPECIAL BONUS

WEEKDAY REFLECTIONS FOR LENT 141
From Ash Wednesday through Wednesday
of Holy Week based on the daily lectionary
readings

Bringing the
WORD
to Life

INTRODUCTION

Bringing the Word to Life: Scripture Messages That Change Lives presents a series of reflections for highly effective living based on the Scripture readings and feasts for Year C of the liturgical cycle. It is offered as a resource for meditative reflection on a weekly and seasonal basis. The Sunday readings and feast days have been examined to glean one specific insight that, if acknowledged and put into practice, could be instrumental in improving the quality of one's life.

God's Word is sent forth to produce an effect on those who hear it. "So shall my word be that goes forth from my mouth; it shall not return to me empty, but it shall accomplish that which I purpose, and prosper in the thing for which I sent it" (Isaiah 55:11). The Word becomes productive, however, only when those who read or hear it see a serviceable connection to the needs of everyday living. The Word "prospers" when it generates life-enhancing shifts in perception and behavioral change. Jesus moved his listeners not only with presentations of eternal spiritual truths, but with deep psychological insights into the workings of the human heart. His preaching confronted mindsets and called for conversion, always in terms of the contemporary settings in which he lived, and always with the view of improving the quality of people's lives. The reflections advanced in this book are offered with the same consideration.

Bringing the Word to Life follows the order of Scripture readings offered in the Roman Catholic and Protestant liturgical year for Sundays and feast days, beginning with the first Sunday of Advent. These readings are plotted out over a three-year period of time (Years A, B, and C) before repeating themselves. Text references are from the Revised Standard Version-

Catholic Edition. Not all readings of a given day have been used for the reflection (feast days are often treated with the theme of the feast itself); those selected for commentary, however, are indicated in bold type. Reflections are presented without repeating or paraphrasing a scriptural passage; the presumption is that the readings indicated in bold type have actually been read.

These reflections are offered to anyone searching for an enhanced quality of life and willing to use the inexhaustible richness of the Word of the Lord as a resource for deeper spirituality. They can be useful to preachers as a source of seminal ideas for sermon topics and development, to Bible study groups searching for ways to make Scripture come "alive," to teachers for classroom use, and also to editors for relevant essay material for parish bulletins and other publications.

For treatment of specific topics, the reader is directed to the table of contents and to Topics and Themes on pages 135-139.

LIVING RIGHTEOUSLY

Most bookstores today have substantial inventories of material dedicated to self-improvement. It is apparent that many people are searching for ways to live a better quality life. It is also apparent that there are many proposals for bringing this about. Formulas are offered for controlling distressing thoughts, getting in touch with feelings, letting go of grievances, accessing the inner child, developing willpower, and the like. The readings today also offer a specific formula for enhanced living. The Word of God is no less concerned with improving the quality of our lives. Each reading in turn suggests a common prescription: righteous living.

We begin a new liturgical year on this first Sunday of Advent with a call from the Scriptures that we commit ourselves to live righteously. The prophet Jeremiah foresees the coming of the Messiah who will "execute justice and righteousness in the land." It is righteousness that will allow Jerusalem to "dwell securely," and "The Lord is our righteousness" will be its new name. Paul exhorts the Thessalonians that they be "unblamable in holiness" by living according to the instructions that he left them. Luke presents Jesus forecasting ominous signs that will preface the coming of redemption, and warning his followers not to be "weighed down with dissipation and drunkenness and the cares of this life."

The theme is clear enough, but what exactly is "righteous living"? In the first place, righteous living is not to be confused with the self-righteousness that Jesus found so deplorable in the attitudes of many of the Pharisees. This kind of righteousness is characterized by an intellectual smugness and hardness of heart that is closed to spiritual growth. No, righteous living can be defined simply as *doing what is right*. Righteous living is behaving in a way that we know is right.

But isn't such a proposition simplistic? After all, what is

"right"? Our society is staggering under confusions about right and wrong. We can find authorities bickering on all sides of pressing moral issues; debates over abortion, for example, or assisted suicide, continue to make front page news. The Word of God, however, calls us to clarity, not confusion. And this clarity relies on the insights and intuitions of a mind and a heart living according to the mind and heart of the Lord to reveal authentic righteousness. Simply put, if we are dedicated to living as true disciples of Christ, we will know what is "right." Love has a remarkable talent for clearing up confusion. If we commit ourselves to live lovingly, we will do what is right whatever the situation or circumstances.

Commit yourself to live righteously. Improve the quality of your life, and grow spiritually, by making it your steadfast intention to always do what is *right*. Before making any decisions that will affect your life, or the lives of others, recollect yourself, say a prayer and ask yourself: "what's the right thing to do here?" Not what's expedient, not what's the easy way out, not what will guarantee a financial payoff, but "What's right?" If you remain unsure or confused, ask yourself: "What would the Lord do in this situation?" "What would a loving person do under these circumstances?" If your heart is identified with the heart of Jesus, you will do the right thing.

DIGGING AT THE ROOTS

Physicians find that a major part of their practice is medicating symptoms of illnesses. Many times patients are reluctant to address the causes behind a sickness, especially if it might suggest a need for some major shift in life-style. Easier to take Mylanta, for example, than explore the underlying reasons of a stressful life. Likewise, mental health professionals often discover that working with a client is little more than "bandaging up" a hurting personality. When the client feels better, he or she usually terminates therapy. A real "cure" would necessitate delving beyond the symptoms of a particular disorder into its roots; not simply learning better control of one's temper, for instance, but discovering what inside is generating so much anger in the first place. But this is something many clients have neither desire nor patience to do. Better a prescription for a tranquilizer than a probe into one's inner soul.

The second Sunday of Advent encourages digging at the roots. All the readings today propose fundamental change. The reading from Baruch senses a radical shift in current events about to unfold, and exhorts the people of Israel to "take off the garment of your sorrow and affliction," and "put on forever the beauty of the glory from God." Paul's letter to the Philippians encourages them to be "pure and blameless" in order that they may fully experience the "day of Christ." An old way of life is to be put aside in order to enjoy the "fruits of righteousness." John the Baptist appears in the gospel of Luke preaching a "baptism of repentance." Preparation for the coming of Christ would require a major change of heart.

Improvement always means change. If we hope for a more productive and happy life, some changes in our life patterns will have to occur. Generally, the deeper the change the better. Developing better relationships, for example, with one's family and friends, may result from being more pleasant, but may also demand spending more quality time with them by cutting down on other commitments. Improving physical health will not only require the avoidance of fattening foods, but a full commitment to proper nutrition and exercise. In terms of spiritual growth, change will often mean something more than cosmetic touch-ups. According to today's readings, growing in the way of the Lord does not discount developing a better prayer life, or performing works of charity, but points to something more radical: a fundamental change of heart. This means going beyond correcting petty faults and bothersome idiosyncracies, and looking deeply at what *drives* us. Not only taking measure of bad language, but of bad attitudes. Not only examining problems, but our priorities. Not only evaluating behavior, but our hearts.

Make this Advent productive by giving serious reflection to important changes you might need to make in your life. Is your relationship with your spouse and family all that it should be? Do you find your work rewarding? Is your health good? Where is there room for improvement? Do certain problems or conflicts constantly repeat themselves? What are they stemming from? Is it faulty attitudes that are always getting you into trouble? Are you in the grip of unworkable beliefs and self-defeating assumptions about yourself and other people? What basically do you need to change? Remember that weeds in your garden are not eliminated by clipping their leaves, but by digging them up by the roots.

JOY IN THE ORDINARY

The prophet Zephaniah and Paul both sound almost ecstatic in today's readings as they proclaim a time for rejoicing. In this season of joy, we might hear this announcement with particular interest. Who of us wouldn't appreciate more joy in our lives? With our own pressing problems, and the never-ending crises facing society, rejoicing isn't a consistent experience. Yes, we hear the call to joy, but the challenge is how to find it on a more permanent basis.

Each of the readings offers an answer to, "How?" Zephaniah reminds us that the Lord is in our midst and "you shall fear evil no more." We are enveloped by the presence of God and showered in God's love. Paul tells us that, "The Lord is at hand," and we need "have no anxiety about anything." If we have needs and problems, we should simply present them to God and then be at peace. The gospel of Luke offers its particular response in an interesting exchange between John the Baptist and the multitudes who have come out to hear him. Who are these people? What are they looking for? These are ordinary people like us, looking for words of comfort, searching for answers to the riddles of life, hoping to find joy in the midst of everyday hassles. They ask the Baptist: "What then shall we do?" And what answer does this great prophet offer? Not a word about more government spending, better education, economic reform, jumping on the bandwagon of one cause or another, or getting therapy. What he says is: share what you have; don't cheat people; don't bully anyone; be content with what you have. Sound rather ordinary? Precisely!

We may have singular moments in life where we experience the excitement of a significant achievement, the ecstasy of sexual union, the rapture of falling in love, and the like, but the greatest teachers of mankind have always taught that if we wish to experience joy on a consistent basis, we need to find it in the ordinary people, places, times, and situations that surround us. But this often has not been part of our training and experience. We await the spectacular and fail to see the wonder in what's ordinary. We look at the big picture and miss the artistry in the fine details. We are awed by oceans but not by a cup of cool water. We marvel over mountains but not over the faces of our loved ones.

According to our readings today, the "secret" of joy is being more aware of the loving presence of God in our lives, allowing this loving God to share our burdens, and living with simple codes of good behavior, "content" with what we have. This should encourage us to know that we are in good hands, and that we should find joy in the ordinary things that surround us. The smile on a child's face. The touch of a wife's hand. A call from a friend. A Christmas tree all lit up with ornaments. The glow of a fire. The smell of roasting turkey. The lights and colors that play off the faces of thousands of people crowding a shopping mall. Ordinary things, in ordinary events, with ordinary people—it's all there, if we only take time to really look.

Eliminate grandiose expectations of what you need to be happy. Take time to notice and appreciate the ordinary things that surround you every day. Meditate on the loving presence of God within you; humbly make your requests known to God. Always be honest and forthright and your joy will not be affected by guilt and shame. Don't lie or cheat, and be content with what you have at the present moment. It will give you all the joy you can handle.

TRUST THE GRAND DESIGN

One of the most important questions we can ever ask ourselves is, "does life have meaning over and above our own designs?" Does life have purpose beyond our making? How we answer this question has significant ramifications for our happiness and peace of mind. Is there a divine blueprint for how life unfolds or are we just random players in a blind universe where everything happens by chance?

Micah is clearly a prophet of the grand design. He announces that God has great plans for the little town of Bethlehem that will have wondrous implications even "to the ends of the earth." The reading from Hebrews assumes that God has great designs for the world in Jesus Christ and encourages our participation in those designs by submission to God's will. Elizabeth, in the reading from Luke, proclaims Mary as "blessed" because of her trust in the fulfillment of God's plans for her.

Believing in a "grand design" or trusting in "the big picture" is not always easy to do. There are times when we are in love, or when everything is going our way, and we feel that all's well in God's world. We may look up into the clear skies on a romantic evening and the dazzle of stars reinforces our belief that, "there must be something behind all this." But there are other times when this belief is severely challenged. Infants die of genetic disorders; children perish in floods or from famine. Innocent bystanders are gunned down by a madman, and calamities befall the most undeserving. We get sick for no reason, lose a job without cause, watch a loved one pine away and die in the prime of life. Life can become so filled up with confusion and problems that all we see is chaos.

And yet we are assured by the readings today that there is a grand design. The problem is we don't want to accept "the big picture" in its entirety. We don't want to believe that God's will embraces the bad with the good, that *everything* that happens is part of God's design, whether we understand how that can be or not. If we accept God's will, however, we need to accept it wholly, without breaking it into pieces according to our particular demands and expectations. We gain great peace of mind when we embrace the belief that there is a divine blueprint for the universe that is good, loving, true, and perfect. Effective living is empowered by a belief that we are part of a "big picture," that there is a purpose and fulfillment for each of us in the grand scheme of things. With Mary we are "blessed" in our trust of that fulfillment. Our joy is increased the more we accept God's will in its fullness. This means that we accept both the sweet and the sour of life as part of God's plan, that even tragedy has its purpose even when it is not presently clear to us what that purpose might be.

As Christmas approaches and we celebrate God's grand design unfolding in the birth of Jesus, trust that God has a grand design for your life too. God willed for you to be, and your life has a special part to play in God's plan. Pray, as did Christ, "Lo, I have come to do thy will, O God." Embrace God's will as fully as you can. Say to yourself often: "Everything in my life has meaning." Everything! You are never a "victim," and nothing happens to you purely by chance. Accept your sorrows as well as your joys, your sufferings as well as your successes, as all part of God's will. Your life continues to unfold as a magnificent drama with God as Director.

BIRTH OF POSSIBILITIES

In a popular talk show, a panel of children was asked: "What do you like most about Christmas?" Many predictably responded that they liked Christmas trees and decorations, time off from school, and especially getting presents. Some of the children, however, responded: "people smile more," "my grandpa who is always sick, gets better," "my mom cooks good food," and "my dad is nice to me." The Christmas season does have a noticeable effect on many people, who act differently than they do at other times of the year. Some are more pleasant and do smile more. Others are more polite, forgiving, generous, and outgoing. We might receive greetings and well-wishes, for example, from neighbors who would not otherwise take note of us. In the spirit of this season, we become aware of possibilities.

Isaiah speaks of "good tidings" and suggests how wondrously different life will be with the coming of God's reign. John's gospel celebrates that "the Word became flesh and dwelt among us," and that, with the Incarnation, we are empowered to become "children of God." The ramifications for an enriched and happier life suggested by these readings are exciting to contemplate. Just think of the possibilities. When Jesus was born, what a vast potential for good lay in that crib of straw; what an impact that birth would have for the development of civilization, for a new moral order, for religion, for art, music, and a new way of looking at human relationships. That first Christmas was a birth of possibilities.

Christmas promotes possibility thinking. Life can be enriched. We can be different and come to experience life more abundantly. Christmas encourages us to be aware of our capacity for change and growth. Life need never be boring, a "drudge," or stagnant because our possibilities are inexhaustible. Unfortunately, we "children of God" rarely reflect on the possibilities offered in our own birth. We become creatures of habit and get "stuck in our ways." Many of us easily give up on ourselves, deny our talents, and become fatalistic about the future. The older we get the more reluctant we are to "get involved." "I can't" becomes a common excuse whenever a suggestion comes up that we try something new. After a while we may even begin believing we have nothing to live for anymore. And that's a sad commentary on how we've allowed life to get away from us. But the fact that we can be so different in this season of the year proves something: there is more to us than meets the eye. There are hints that possibilities still lie dormant within us.

The joy of life is in living! If you have "things to do and places to go," your energy level will remain high and life will be vibrant. Give yourself a Christmas gift this year and replace "I can't" with possibility thinking. Stop thinking small of yourself and don't be afraid to take some risks. What is still waiting to be born in you? Do you have talents that you've neglected over the years? Can you sing, dance, tell good stories, make people laugh? What dreams of your childhood are still awaiting fulfillment? Take time to make them come alive. What can you do to make a better life for the people around you? What can you do to bring more joy to your spouse, your children, and friends? There is vast potential in all of us waiting for its chance to see the light of day. Have your own "blessed event" this Christmas and allow some of it to be born.

SEAT OF LEARNING

Statistics provide ample evidence of the impact of stable family life, or the lack thereof, on the well-being of society. It can be shown, for example, that children from healthy home environments are likely to have good self-esteem, do well in school, and exhibit good social skills. On the other hand, it can be demonstrated that there is a direct correlation between broken homes and the crime rate. The quality of family life has repercussions on a child's ability to develop moral standards, set goals, and enter into gratifying relationships. A dysfunctional family can scar and handicap a child for life.

The feast of the Holy Family takes note of the fact that Jesus was born into a family. Historically, the church has consistently offered the Holy Family as a model for Christian family living. Why is this so? In the gospel reading, Luke comments that Jesus "increased in wisdom and in stature, and in favor with God and men." There is every reason to believe that Jesus developed the way he did because of his learning experiences in family life. Jesus was influenced in his personality traits, feelings, hopes, and aspirations by the training and interactions he experienced at home.

While many authors today view family as an endangered species, even expendable, family life continues to remain the primary seat of learning, the most important learning institution in the world. Early life training in family stays with us for life. Nowhere is our character more deeply fashioned, our basic belief system more inflexibly developed, our fundamental feelings about God, life, and the world more deeply imprinted. How we experience love from our parents, for example, affects the way we tend to love others. The kind of affirmation and support we receive has impact on our ambitions, motivation, and our ability to handle our problems. It all begins in the home.

One of the most pressing needs of our time is for family life to be pursued more deliberately—with more awareness of what kind of learning is going on. Family is not something we just fall into, it is something we consciously create. Together with aunts and uncles, brothers and sisters, cousins and grandparents, family is something we *work* at. The primary "work" of family is teaching. Parents, for example, provide their children with a powerful model of devoted love by the way they work through their marital problems. Grandparents give witness to the benefits of commitment, loyalty, wisdom, and perseverance. Relationships with cousins often offer us our first intimations of our interconnectedness with the broader spectrum of humanity. With a safe and accepting home environment children are encouraged to be themselves and experiment with their dreams without ridicule and put-downs.

> Many successful businesspeople lament: "I wish I had spent more time with my family." Don't allow this remorse to one day be your own. Invest in your family. What obligations to other family members are you neglecting? What kind of modeling do you provide? Do you need to spend more quality time with your loved ones, or be more supportive? Is your home a safe haven where family members feel unconditionally loved and accepted? Tell your children how lovable they are. Make a point of doing things as a family. Family is the best investment you will ever make.

HOSPITALITY

The holiday season is noted for its hospitality. Office parties are common. We have family gatherings for extravagant meals and the exchange of gifts. Out-of-town guests may arrive and we welcome them warmly into our homes to partake in our festivities. We share greetings with one another as we do at no other time of the year. We even decorate our houses with lights and special ornamentation to suggest that our homes are filled with happiness and good cheer that we wish for everyone. Hopefully, this is true.

In the gospel reading, Luke presents a short narrative about shepherds coming to visit Mary and her baby. It must have been a memorable visit because the shepherds left glorifying God for the wonders they had seen. We can only imagine the welcome Mary offered the shepherds as she showed them her son and exchanged wonderful stories with them. And this is how Mary would forever be remembered. Christians throughout the centuries have seen her as a model of hospitality. Paintings and statues of Mary usually present her with arms open wide in welcome.

There is something eminently grace-filled about hospitality. Have we ever walked into a home where we felt genuinely welcomed? Where we were put immediately at ease with an encouragement to "make yourself at home"? Have there been times when we gathered with old friends and their faces lit up with excitement at seeing us? There is power in hospitality. It makes us feel loved. It frees us to be ourselves, without formalities, or the need to put on a show. It's a wonderful feeling and we rarely forget it.

Can we imagine what neighborhoods would be like with more evidence of hospitality? What our workplaces would be like? What world conditions would be like if nations were more hospitable to one another? Think of how racial tensions and ethnic intolerance would diminish if hospitality were more a rule of life. Consider how much more meaningful our worship services would be if churches were dedicated havens of welcome. The book of Numbers records a beautiful blessing: "The Lord bless you and keep you: The Lord make his face to shine upon you, and be gracious to you: The Lord lift up his countenance upon you, and give you peace." This blessing is more than a pious piece of poetry; it suggests a frame of mind. Our calling, and joy, as Christians is to bless people with our own graciousness. This means maintaining an attitude of accepting people just as they are, and letting them know that they, and their needs, are important to us. This, of course, may not always be easy to do, but it certainly provides us with opportunity for a wonderful New Year's resolution—that we be hospitable in our dealings with everyone.

Make a New Year's resolution to open your heart to others. Remember that people generally perform according to your expectations of them. Enemies, for example, are usually made, not found. Get to know more people in the community where you worship. Keep a smile on your face and willingly offer your services to those in need. What can you do to make your home a place where everyone can feel at home? Can you be more cordial when people ask you for directions, or more agreeable when a fellow worker asks you for help? Think of Mary and her open arms. You are blessed and can afford to bless in return.

CHILD OF GREAT PROMISE

Matthew's gospel recounts the story of wise men following a magical star that led them to the newborn Christ child. Arriving at their destiny, the story goes, they fell down in worship and offered gifts of gold, frankincense, and myrrh. Gifts of such extravagance are befitting an infant predestined for an eminent destiny. For the wise men, this was a child of great promise.

Let us take a moment and go back in imagination to the moment of our own birth. After nine months cradled in the nurturing comfort of a womb, we probably came into the world with much fanfare. A child's birth is a "blessed event." For parents, it is a moment of great joy. Perhaps we were the answer to a mother's prayer, the fulfillment of a father's hope. Whatever the expectation, our birth was a moment of wonder. It is no surprise, therefore, that when a newborn infant is first placed into its mother's arms, she not only gazes in excitement at her own little "miracle," but wishes the best and fullest of life for her child. She might even forecast great things for its future. Every mother has great dreams for her children. In a mother's eye, her child is born for an eminent destiny. Each of us is born as a child of great promise.

We're aware, however, perhaps painfully so, that life has a tendency to modify dreams and renege on promises. Disappointments take their toll and we tend to become resigned to an accommodation with life. Many of us go through our adult lives in rather humdrum fashion. We have our daily routines, make sure our insurance premiums are paid up, and hope that no serious misfortune disturbs our hard-earned comforts. Much of our time is spent reacting to what life throws our way rather than proactively setting new goals for ourselves. Our golden rule is often quite defensive: "don't bother me, and I won't bother you."

Epiphany, however, is a gentle reminder of our specialness. It asks us to recall the great promise we were born with. Epiphany encourages us not to forsake the promise because of our pain, and not to lose heart in the face of our problems. We are asked to rediscover our mother's dreams for us and to evaluate how many of them have come true. No matter what the unfolding of our life, none of us ever ceases to be a person of destiny, a child of great promise. In the reading from Ephesians, Paul reminds us that we are "partakers of the promise of Christ." Until the day we die—and beyond—the promise remains in force. We may never attain fame and fortune, but that will never discount the fact that we were born to be special, to do something special, to make a special contribution to life.

Ask your mother what her dreams were for you on the day you were first placed in her arms. Can you appreciate how much you were a child of great promise? Is life still full of promise, or have you become cynical over time and expect less and less of your life? Are your eyes focused on the future or do you still live a lot in the past? Do you believe in your possibilities? It's one thing to be "realistic," but do you usually settle for the mediocre in your work performance and relationships? God always loves you as you are, and you are always special no matter your successes or failings—but God also invites you to become all you can be. From the words of the prophet Isaiah, "Arise, shine; for your light has come." You are made to shine in excellence. Why settle for less?

DEVELOPING RESOURCES

Our culture is characterized by its extraordinary pace of life. Many of us feel we are riding in a whirlwind. It's astonishing how quickly one season passes before we find ourselves in another. If we are like most people, we are always busy, busy, busy. There never seems to be enough time to do what we need to do. As a result of this rapid pace of life, we often feel worn out and drained. Millions today complain of "burnout." A good night's sleep, even a couple weeks of vacation, doesn't seem enough to restore us to our old vim and vigor.

A fast-paced life, however, appears here to stay. It's unlikely that demands on our time from career, family, maintenance chores, and the like are going to dwindle significantly. Most of us don't have the option of being able to retire early, get away from family responsibilities, pursue a less demanding job, or go off to a monastery. Which leads to a consideration of resources: what keeps us going? Too few people are actively engaged in pursuing resources for personal renewal. And with dire consequences. We can own the most luxurious car in the world, loaded with maximum horsepower and every premium option that a manufacturer can provide, but if there is no gas in the tank, the car is not going anywhere. Without "fuel" for an accelerated pace of life, we soon run ourselves into the ground.

The readings today attest to the importance of Spirit as an indispensable resource. Isaiah outlines the work to be done by God's special servant and is assured that the work will be accomplished, because "I have put my Spirit upon him." The reading from Acts notes that the mission of Jesus is being accomplished because "God anointed Jesus of Nazareth with the Holy Spirit and with power." Luke quotes John the Baptist welcoming the coming of Christ and remarking that his followers would receive from him a special baptism "with the Holy Spirit and with fire." If we inquire as to the nature of this

"Spirit," we are led to conclude from the readings that it is *energy*.

Few things are more important to living fully and productively than finding resources that can energize us. It is energy that keeps us going, and we owe it to ourselves to find plentiful resources for renewing that energy. The gospel suggests that Jesus found an enormous resource for his ministry in the love he felt from God: "Thou art my beloved Son; with thee I am well pleased." Setting aside a few moments every day to communicate with God can do wonders to uplift our spirits. And there are other resources. Scheduling time to read, meditate, go on retreat, relax with family, have fun with friends, can go a long way toward renewing us. Making time for unrushed meals, good nutrition, and regular exercise can contribute significantly to restoring our energy levels.

> Having a full and busy life is not bad as long as you find resources for renewing your energy. Are you aware of your resources? When you feel "on empty," what fills you up? Make time every day to refuel yourself. Replenish your spirit with worship, prayer, inspiring reading, healthy eating habits, humor, regular exercise, rest, and creative hobbies. Contemplate God's unconditional love for you and relish the love you receive from a spouse, your family, and friends. Resources are indispensable for effective living and should be pursued as deliberately as anything else that is important in your life.

ASH WEDNESDAY
Joel 2:12–18 **2 Corinthians 5:20–6:2** Matthew 6:1–6, 16–18

NOW IS
THE ACCEPTABLE TIME

Most of us tend to procrastinate. It is a weakness of human nature that we put important things off. We delay making an appointment with the dentist, starting much needed repairs on the roof, or giving up a nasty habit. And procrastination is usually costly. The toothache gets worse, the leaking roof causes extensive interior damage, and the bad habit takes a devastating toll on our health. Putting things off for the future also sets us up with a "someday" complex. Some of us are always talking about "someday." "Someday I'll travel the world." "Someday when I get married, I'll be happy." "Someday, when the children are raised, I'll have time for myself." "Someday, when I retire, I'll take more time for my spiritual development." But, alas, it is a sad fact that "someday" often never comes.

This is exactly what seems to concern Paul in his letter to the Corinthians. He writes to people who were looking for salvation. He encourages them to "be reconciled to God," that they might "become the righteousness of God." He entreats them "not to accept the grace of God in vain," by failing to incorporate that grace into their daily living. Any temptation to procrastinate is put off with an emphatic "Behold, now is the acceptable time; behold, now is the day of salvation." Don't look toward tomorrow for what is already available to us right here and now.

Living NOW is an attitude of soul. Eliminating procrastination requires disciplined concentration on the present. Unfortunately, many of us make a habit of living in the past by lamenting lost opportunities, thinking about how times were better before, blaming others for our predicaments, hanging onto guilt, and constantly berating ourselves for past mistakes.

Others, on the other hand, live in the future, always making big plans with no commitment to action, hoping for a better quality life with no strategies for achieving it—all the while ignoring present possibilities and the blessings of the moment.

NOW is the only reality that is. Yes, we have a past, but it is only in memory. There is a future, but it exists only in imagination. NOW is what *is*! It is important to set goals, but we also need to take advantage of the graces available to us right now. Now is the time to do what we need to do to take care of ourselves. Now is the time to build a better marriage and family life. Now is the time to make that call, make that apology, get rid of that bad habit, say "thank you" for that favor. Today, Ash Wednesday, is the time to be reconciled with God and to begin living righteously. There is no better time than this beginning of Lent to evaluate our spiritual needs and begin to meet them.

Make this your best Lent ever. Begin your journey to Easter with a commitment to live fully with the graces of the present moment. No more recriminations over the past, no procrastination about doing what you need to do to take care of yourself today. See in the ashes you receive an old style of life dying and a new style being born. Take advantage of every day of Lent to grow spiritually. What would help give you the kind of life your loving God wishes for you? What is preventing you from being righteous in God's eyes? Make a resolution and begin today. "Now is the acceptable time."

Personal Allegiance to Jesus

Rarely a month goes by that the media doesn't present us with exciting news of a medical breakthrough or some major advance in technology. Scientific progress is heralding undreamed-of possibilities for human achievement. Nevertheless, prophets of doom abound as we edge our way toward a new millennium. The media also present us with daily accounts of unrelenting human misery. Some social critics are convinced that we are witnessing a collapse of society. Breakdowns in values once held sacred are alarming. We can't avoid being affected by a widespread perception that "everything is falling apart." Our own faith and values may be in a state of confusion. Perhaps we despair: "I don't know what to believe any more." Where everything is "up in the air," there results a dramatic toll on our sense of stability, self-esteem, and purposefulness, not to mention our happiness. Millions of people today are conscious of a great moral vacuum in their lives.

Not that there aren't marketers willing to fill the void—even in Luke's gospel we see the devil presenting Jesus with all kinds of suggestions for how he should fulfill his destiny. Never in history have there been so many hawkers of happiness scrambling for our attention. All of us have a deep need for wisdom and guidance, especially in troublesome times, and we're more than willing to listen to formulas for successful living. The sad fact is, however, that these formulas are often little more than trendy enticements, and the get-rich-quick scheme ends up costing us money. It's difficult not to become even more confused and disillusioned. Where can we Christians turn, therefore, to find a more promising foundation for living at our best?

In his letter to the Romans, Paul unreservedly asserts that our only hope of real salvation in this life is wholehearted acceptance of Jesus as "the Lord." It is important we understand what this means in practical terms. Paul is speaking about developing a special allegiance to Jesus. This means giving Jesus and his teachings a place of primacy in our lives. For Paul, Jesus is the only teacher, guru, model, and guide we will ever need. We need to hear Paul out. Even from the most secular of perspectives, the teachings of Jesus are unrivaled for their sublimity and simplicity in offering nurture to the hungers of the human heart. Jesus offers no exercises, no techniques, no quick fixes, and yet, "everyone who calls upon the name of the Lord will be saved." Paul asserts personal allegiance to Jesus as the answer to our searching for a better and happier life. As we journey through Lent, therefore, we need to study Jesus more closely, examine the style of life he models, hear his words with fresh awareness. The Word of God is eternal, and will never go out of fashion. If Jesus is the Word of God come into this world, his message deserves more than a casual hearing. It is our allegiance to Jesus himself that brings us salvation. In thought, word, and deed, we need to think more with the mind of Christ in the way we meet our situations and deal with other people.

Ask the Lord to come into your life. Address him as "Lord" and ask him for guidance as you go about your daily affairs. Read the Scriptures with a mind to making practical applications of what moves you. When you hear the Word of the Lord at worship, always inquire: "What is this reading trying to tell me?"... "What lesson is there for me here?" Give full allegiance to Jesus as the Lord of your life, and you will find not only your true purpose, but everything you need to fulfill it.

ABLE TO SEE

Today's gospel narrative presents the story of Jesus' "transfiguration." Taking along a few close friends, Jesus goes off to a mountain to pray. While he is at prayer, a remarkable event takes place: the physical appearance of Jesus changes dramatically and the disciples "saw his glory." Christians traditionally interpret this event as Jesus revealing his divinity to his disciples. But we miss an important point here if we fail to see that there is another side to this revelation. True, Jesus may have revealed his divine nature, but what is significant is something revealed about the disciples themselves: they were able to see it. These chosen friends of the Lord had reached a point in their spiritual development where they were able to *perceive* divinity.

Let us try to see the implications of this passage for us. An artist and a groundskeeper have different perspectives when they look out at a lawn spread over many acres. The artist may see a landscape worthy of a canvas and set out to buy brushes and paints for his palette. The groundskeeper may see a monotonous job ahead of cutting grass, trimming trees, and pulling weeds. Needless to say, they will approach their tasks with different enthusiasm. The artist can look at an ordinary tree, even a weed, and see something of beauty. The artist has an ability to see beauty from heightened awareness and a refined inner vision.

Living a happier and more enhanced life depends to a great extent on how well we sensitize ourselves and refine our ability to see. There is so much wonder and beauty in the world around us that completely escapes our attention. There are people around us every day who are remarkably kind, considerate, humorous, and loving. It may be hidden under a businesslike demeanor, but it's there. Each of us has talent and graciousness that we often hide from ourselves. We become so concerned with putting on shows to please others that we neglect to see the real beauty that lies within us. Furthermore, God is there to be revealed in the ordinary events of our day, in nature, in the smiles of friends, and in the faces of our loved ones. A lovely poem calls attention to the fact that "the world is charged with the grandeur of God"—if only we have the presence of soul to see.

It's a fact that we see what we want to see. But it's also a fact that we see what we are taught to see. Many artists have natural talent, but many more are meticulously trained in their craft. We can *learn* to see goodness and beauty in other people, and in ourselves. With more determined focus, for example, we can perceive divinity shining through the face of a stranger. God is all, and in all. God does not hide from us. God is there, everywhere, to be seen. Our joyous task as Christians is not only to be more Christlike but to become more visionary—like those first disciples who "saw his glory."

Are you willing to get beyond your present perceptions and prejudices, and really see? "If you look for trouble," the saying goes, "you will find it," but, by the same token, if you look for good, you will find it too. There is good in everybody. There is something good to be learned even from pain and misfortune. Are you willing to look? Open your eyes of faith. See God's will in all the events of your life. See God's presence in members of your family, in the people you work with or encounter in the street. God wants to be obvious. Can you see?

SECOND CHANCE

There is a short parable told in the gospel reading that is very intriguing. It talks about getting a second chance. A fig tree did not bear fruit for three years and its owner decided to cut it down. But a vinedresser intervened to give it another chance to produce. If it still didn't bear fruit after more caring, it would be cut down. Jesus offers an important lesson here. Few of us can get through a day without making mistakes, sometimes serious mistakes, in the decisions we make, in the way we handle people, or in how we carry out our responsibilities. None of us is perfect; we make errors in judgment and performance. The mistakes we make, of course, have consequences. Penalties await our blunders. But if we have a mature sense of responsibility, we take our lickings, pay our dues, and settle our debts. And then we get on with life.

It often happens, however, that a cause doesn't result in its predictable effect, an error doesn't reap its appropriate penalties. Somehow grace intervenes and saves us from dire consequences. For example, we might be driving well over the speed limit when we catch sight of a state trooper's car hidden in a bay of an overpass. A rush of adrenaline convinces us that we are caught. However, a mile passes, then another, and we are not pursued. With a grateful sigh of relief we know we've escaped a rightful ticket. Experiences such as this are common. By the skin of our teeth, we just avoid a serious accident that could have resulted from our lack of concentration. A potentially deadly skin cancer, the result of many long hours in the sun, responds favorably to treatment. A spouse whom we have hurt with neglect or abusive language brushes it off with forgiveness on the spot. We get a reprieve. We may even feel we "got away with murder."

The message of the parable, however, is a little more positive. It encourages us to *take advantage* of our second chances—that we accept them not as mere strokes of good luck, but as graces to learn something. There are important lessons in life we can learn without having to endure the customary pain. It all depends on whether or not we can accept the grace of a reprieve, and run with it. If, after getting a reprieve, we go on with the same risky habits, the same poor choices, the same bad behavior, we prove only that we are ungrateful for having been spared. We have learned nothing and will eventually get "cut down." And who can we blame but ourselves? A man who goes back to smoking after a part of his lung is removed is not indulging a pleasure, he is choosing to commit suicide.

It is part of life's process that we get our "licks," but we also get our "breaks." Consider the times you were spared the penalties for bad behavior or poor performance. Have you been abusive to others, for example, where they forgave you and took you back? Do you have addictive habits that can be stopped before they irreparably harm you physically or emotionally? Have you been spared answering for criminal activity? Can you feel gratitude for the grace of a second chance? What will you do to ensure a mistake will not be repeated? If you don't want to fall into the category of people who "just never learn," use your "breaks" to your advantage. When you get a second chance, take it.

GRACE OF FORGIVENESS

Jesus' parable of the prodigal son is one of the most beautiful and meaningful parables in all the gospels. The reading from Luke today touches us deeply because it addresses forgiveness, both divine and human. The parable is complex and considers forgiveness from a number of angles. It is a revelation of God's manner of forgiving our offenses: complete and absolute. Jesus confirms that God holds no grudges and embraces us with indescribable love and mercy, no matter what we have done. The father of the prodigal neither rejects nor reprimands his son; he throws him a feast. For anyone burdened with problems of remorse and guilt, this should be music to their ears. The parable is also an example of the wisdom of self-forgiveness. The prodigal son "came to his senses," repented, and returned home. What this urges us to do is take full responsibility for our decisions and actions, and come to terms with their consequences. We get on with our lives, and live effectively, not by making excuses for ourselves, or bemoaning our mistakes, but by forgiving ourselves and then doing our best to make amends. We make amends best by "returning home" and living with more mature understanding. Last, this parable stands out as an indictment of lack of forgiveness, as demonstrated in the brother who did not share his father's compassion for the wayward brother. We are duly warned that not forgiving others comes with its own particular penalties.

Accepting that God forgives us absolutely can do wonders to raise the level of our peace of mind. It is also rebukes the occasional arrogance that may arise that "God could never forgive me for that." What would ever make us think God could not forgive us? This parable disallows us from making God "small." Furthermore, if God is so forgiving, why would we ever dream of withholding forgiveness from ourselves? We have no need to drag along the baggage of guilt that is potentially so devastating to happy and productive living. Forgiving ourselves, for whatever our mistakes, allows us to pick ourselves up when we fall and carry on with our lives without looking back.

By the same token, of course, we are encouraged to be just as forgiving of others. But this kind of forgiving is often the most difficult to do. Most of us live with a fantasy that maintaining our indignation is a way of punishing someone else. Like the unforgiving brother in today's parable we harbor our resentments and hold on to our grievances and never seem to realize that we are hurting no one but ourselves. Think of the relationships that are shattered, families that are broken up, and whole societies that are ravaged by wars of vengeance, all because grudges are maintained and nurtured. The foolishness that parades around as "teaching them a lesson" staggers the imagination. No one suffers more from a grudge than the one who bears it.

Are you ready for peace of mind that can last a lifetime? Open your heart to forgiveness. Forgiveness from a loving God, forgiveness for yourself, and forgiveness for others, no matter how they might have offended you. There are few better channels to excellence in life than a compassionate and loving heart. Think of the misery you cause yourself by lack of forgiveness. Consider how many months, if not years, of anguish you endure by maintaining and nurturing your resentments. Forgiveness is a wide door to freedom. It is a door you should want to open every chance you get.

BUT FOR THE
GRACE OF GOD

The gospel reading is not only an example of the Lord's great compassion, it is a short, but classic, study in hypocrisy. A woman caught in adultery is presented to Jesus before she is to be stoned to death. The Pharisees hope Jesus will make some comment that will put him at odds with the law. It is immediately noteworthy that there is no mention of her partner in adultery. Apparently men were not held to the same standards of law. Furthermore, it is quite obvious from the turn of events in this story that those with the heaviest burdens of their own sins were the first in line to throw stones at her. That is, until Jesus exposed their hypocrisy.

We human beings can be strange at times. We say that we can't stand hypocrites and yet there is a strong hypocritical streak in all of us. People, for example, who deplore the "trash" in daily tabloids don't seem to have any reluctance in buying them. We often take pride in being able to spot "a phony," but seem unable to see phoniness in ourselves. Perhaps we feel we are only being "honest" when we point out the faults of others, and yet we become outraged when someone points out one of our faults. How many hours do we spend gossiping about gossips? It is a fact known to psychologists that people most ready to condemn others are generally those trying to hide their own guilt. What's implied is that we try to distract from our own sins by decrying those of others. Some televangelists, for example, exposed for sexual misconduct, are a case in point. Psychologists can also demonstrate that we normally only spot faults in others that we, in some form, carry within ourselves. As the saying goes, "it takes one to know one."

Given the right circumstances, there are few temptations in this world that we might not succumb to. We share a human nature noted for both its wisdom and its failings. With Paul in his letter to the Philippians we can openly admit our lack of perfection. While it is our destiny, and even our desire, to strive for excellence, we do well to be alert to own weaknesses, and the hypocrisy we are tempted to employ to cover them up. Furthermore, we do well to be more understanding. We have no need to expect perfection of ourselves, but we have no right to expect perfection in others either. Our disappointments, stress, and anger over others would be diminished significantly if we could only accept our common humanity. We all make mistakes. We hurt other people, and they hurt us. This doesn't mean that we condone immoral or inappropriate behavior, only that we generally need to have more compassion. "There, but for the grace of God, go I."

Do you take pleasure in scandal? Do you find yourself smugly self-satisfied when the media reports the fall of a popular movie star or political figure? Are you more than ready to engage in gossip about a fellow worker, or more than willing to criticize another family member? What faults are you hiding? Is it possible that any self-right-eousness you have is a cover-up? Let people be. Walk away from negative gossip. Never rebuke a child without first pointing out some good quality you've observed. When you are certain that you are without sin, feel free to pick up stones to cast at others—but not before! Consider the times you felt blessed to be forgiven for some failing. Be willing to extend that same favor to others.

THE NAME OF JESUS

Today we celebrate remembrance of the triumphal entrance of Jesus into Jerusalem. He is met by the multitude waving palm branches and proclaiming "Hosanna" to his name. Paul writes passionately in his letter to the Philippians in praise of the sacrifice of Jesus who "emptied himself, taking the form of a servant." Paul then says that God exalted Jesus and "bestowed on him the name which is above every name, that at the name of Jesus every knee should bow." The name of Jesus, therefore, has had great historical impact. For Christians, the name of Jesus is of singular importance. But what's in a name?

Names have power to affect us. They evoke a response in us, especially if we have a relationship with the one who bears the name. The name of a popular movie star, for example, can cause heart palpitations in adoring fans. Think of how our mother's name can move us emotionally, or how the name of someone we love can bring forth a rush of wonderful memories and sentiments. On the other hand, a name can bring about feelings of anxiety. The name of a tyrant, for instance, can arose fear in a family, or a whole population.

It used to be a practice of Roman Catholics to nod their heads at the mention of the name of Jesus. This was to indicate love and utter respect for the Holy Name. But the name of Jesus has not always evoked a loving image. Jesus has often been perceived, and preached, as judgmental and condemning. Historians note that, "in the name of Jesus," innocent people have been murdered and whole nations have been persecuted. Many envision Jesus separating "the sheep from the goats," sending some to bliss in heaven, and others to the pains of hell. We can only imagine how many have been alienated from churches because of the heavy moralizing often associated with the name of Christ.

People in pain, confusion, or the throes of addiction are not motivated, much less healed, by moralism and judgment. "The name which is above every other name" should never be contrived to bring additional burdens to a soul already overtaxed with suffering. Christianity is a religion of "salvation." Redemption is not brought about through castigations of "sinners." Any condemnations in the name of Jesus rob that holy name of its grace-filled power to save. Paul emphasizes that Jesus "took on the form of a servant." Not a master, judge, or executioner, but a servant. The name of Jesus is "the name above every other name" because it is the name of unconditional love and mercy. It is through unqualified acceptance of us that Jesus brings us salvation. The name of Jesus, therefore, should evoke immediate responses of delight, peace, and encouragement.

What response does the name of Jesus evoke in you? Does it bring you fear or joy? Does it, perhaps, bring apathy? Have you allowed Jesus and the power of his holy name to become distant from you? Do you need to build your relationship with the Lord? The Lord is our salvation. Don't miss out on what unconditional love from Jesus can do to enhance your healing and the quality of your life. Turn to him and invoke the power of his name. The Lord is a servant and takes particular delight in serving you and your needs.

GATHERING OF FRIENDS

Holy Thursday commemorates the Lord's last supper with his disciples. In truth, they were more than disciples to Jesus; they had become his close friends. On the day before he died, Jesus felt a need to gather with his friends. There is nothing in this world more powerful than loving friendship. We will never find a greater source of strength in facing the challenges of life than the presence of supportive friends. A mathematical law is transcended when friends gather together—the whole becomes greater than the sum of its parts. Friendship raises us up from our individuality into the world of community.

A church remains only an impersonal institution, a cold monument of brick and stone, unless it embodies community. Community is not simply people with common goals and interests. People who get together to play bridge, for example, are a club, not a community. What makes "community" is a heritage that professes common beliefs and practices, deep bonding, and visible evidence of love and caring. The readings speak of such community. Exodus describes the rituals of Passover. To this day, Jews continue to remind themselves of those significant events in their history that bind them together in an extraordinary way. Paul, in his letter to the Corinthians, reminds them of the imperishable bond that unites them in the body and blood of Christ. The gospel narrative describes a scene of love and caring that cannot help but move us. Jesus not only gathers for a last supper with his friends, he washes their feet. What are we to learn from such a touching display of intimacy, especially when Jesus makes clear, "For I have given you an example, that you also should do as I have done to you"?

Church communities can become fictitious if the elements of community are not sensed and expressed. Liturgies can be sterile rituals unless a transcendental bond is recognized among worshipers. If our assemblies are not "gatherings of friends," we retain only pale reenactments of the Lord's supper. Any arrogance, aloofness, estrangement, bickering, divisiveness, lack of reconciliation, and the like extinguishes the spirit of community. We need also keep in mind that community never happens by itself, it must be worked at. Churches need more than a united front of doctrinal beliefs and moral values. History demonstrates that "united fronts" often do little more than divide communities with rancor and prejudice. It is love that unites, not a creed. Jesus, for example, did not encourage his friends to adhere to a particular school of thought, he washed their feet. Holy Thursday, therefore, is a reminder not only of our common heritage, but of the charge laid upon us by the example of the Lord to build community in our churches. We need regular assessments of the level of love that exists in our membership. We cannot take each other for granted, much less exist as strangers to one another. There is enormous power in a gathering of friends. It helped the Lord through his Passion, and it can help us through any we might endure.

What are your expectations of the church to which you belong? Are you searching for community? What level of love can be observed among church members? Do you sense a welcoming atmosphere, acceptance, forgiveness, reconciliation, and support? What about your own commitment to community? Can you imagine yourself washing the feet of others, if not literally, at least in terms of service that you are willing to offer to others? Show that you care in the way you greet others; offer a sign of peace from your heart. The example of Jesus is clear.

OVERCOME EVIL
WITH GOOD

No matter how many times we read the Passion of Jesus, it's difficult not to be moved by the tragedy involved in his suffering and death. We witness the naked power of evil and it horrifies us. We might wonder why Christians call this Friday "Good." The drama of the passion and death of Jesus is so moving because it is not a mythical play or well-composed fiction. We witness human nature as it really presents itself, with real people, doing real things, in real life situations. The Passion presents jealous priests who are irate over Jesus' growing popularity, fickle crowds more motivated by spectacle than the pursuit of truth, witnesses lying under oath at a public trial. We observe Pilate making life and death decisions on the basis of political expediency, soldiers just "doing their job," friends of Jesus who betray, deny, and abandon him. In many respects it's a dismal soap opera many of us experience, in part, every day. If this is an accurate commentary on the dark side of human nature, how can we hope to put things right?

There is great popular appeal to a frontal attack on evil. We are easily persuaded that evil must be squarely faced and dealt with. There is always popular support for war "to end all wars," for a "war against crime," for capital punishment, for attacking those who offend us. And yet the attitude of Jesus is far removed from such strategies. Jesus remains consistent in his humble role of servant. He surrenders to the authorities without struggle, and endures trial without uttering a word in his defense. Never does he lash out at his accusers, or point out the illogic or illegality of the trial's proceedings. He carries his own cross to Calvary and dies forgiving his executioners. Jesus was not ignorant, nor was he a pushover. We know he freely accepted the path of his passion and death. What can we Christians learn from this about handling evil?

The teachings and final witness of Jesus tell us that love and forgiveness are the only real remedies for the evils of this world. Evil is not overcome by a showdown. We don't make peace by going to war. Crime will not be reduced by bigger police forces and longer prison terms. Building bigger weapons will not make us feel safer. Nobody is open to seeing things differently unless they are embraced by goodness. Until we bask in the sunshine of love, we never feel comfortable with the risk of making changes. Evil draws strength from resistance; it is empowered by the very forces that seek to attack it. In the presence of goodness and love, evil simply collapses. Jesus provides us with one of the most powerful lessons for peace and productive living: overcome evil with good, conquer hatred with love. Today is "Good" Friday because it celebrates the absolute power of goodness to conquer evil, not by counterattack, but by its sheer presence. Darkness will always be dispelled by the smallest of lights.

What is your usual approach in handling your problems, difficult people, an unexpected illness, a death in the family? Do you rage and carry on as if you've been personally assaulted? What are your beliefs about ending war, bringing down the crime rate, erasing racial tensions, dealing with people who belligerently oppose your views? As you look upon Jesus on the cross, consider his witness. Is it possible that there is another approach to reducing evil in the world, and in your life? Can you believe that good can conquer evil? Let the mind of Christ be your mind, if even for a day. Test the power of your own love and goodness to bring peace to a trying situation.

LIGHT AT THE END
OF THE TUNNEL

Debate continues about the resurrection of Jesus. Did Jesus literally come back from the dead? Is the resurrection only a myth, or worse, a hoax? Did Jesus arise physically in his earthly body or did he rise as a spirit? While polemics may go on forever, they cannot eclipse the fundamental belief of Christians, stated in the reading from the Acts of the Apostles, that God "raised him on the third day and made him manifest." Jesus was raised from the dead. We believe this, however it happened. The "physics" involved in the resurrection are immaterial. What is important for us is that the seemingly catastrophic passion and death of Jesus ended on a happy note. Out of despair came hope, out of darkness came light, out of defeat came glory, out of death came life.

Psychologists note that people can bear almost anything as long as there is some meaning attached to it. We can put up with any "what" as long as we have a "why." Psychologists also observe that people can get through their problems and sufferings much more easily and productively if they believe there is light at the end of the tunnel. And this is precisely the good news that Easter gives us today. The dramatic lesson about Easter is not only that Jesus was raised from the dead, but that the resurrection of Jesus is *our* resurrection. A divine revelation is given that no matter what we suffer, no matter how badly we have it, no matter what tragedies we face—even death itself— we will be raised up as well. There is always light for us at the end of the tunnel.

This light is often difficult to see, even imagine, especially when we are in the grip of an affliction or depression. When there seems to be no end to our struggles, when every road we take comes to a dead end, when suffering continues unabated, our inclination is not to believe in the light, but to curse the darkness. But it is expressly then, Easter promises, in the darkest night of our soul, that our resurrection is closest at hand. It may take great courage, but Easter beckons us to raise our eyes in hope and wait with trust for our redemption. No matter what we endure, God will raise us up. This is the glory of Christianity: the absolute promise of deliverance.

Wisdom tells us there is a silver lining in every cloud, a reason for every problem we face, and an important lesson we need to learn in every suffering we endure. We are told "God never closes a door without opening up another." This isn't wishful thinking but a fact well-supported by experience. Some of the most important steps in our growth have taken place through suffering, which at the time seemed meaningless. There is never a Good Friday, however, without its Easter. Easter affirms that we will never be abandoned, that nothing is ever hopeless. Our strength, therefore, in facing our afflictions is not rigid stoicism, or anger at life, or "why me?", or resignation to fate, but a patient, peaceful, confident Easter belief that it will be OK. There is light at the end of the tunnel.

Affirm your belief in the risen Jesus. Absorb the lesson of his resurrection. Know there is light at the end of the tunnel whether you presently see it or not. When you feel depressed and overcome with hardship, say with all your heart: " I am not abandoned; I will get through this; I know that my Redeemer lives."

SECOND SUNDAY OF EASTER
Acts 5:12–16 Revelation 1:9–11a, 12–13, 17–19 **John 20:19–31**

FAITH PEOPLE

"Faith," like "Love," has a hundred definitions. It means different things for different people. Some look at faith as a form of
trust, taking people at their word. We have faith, for example,
that our physician makes an accurate diagnosis of an illness.
Some see faith as an act of self-confidence. An Olympic diver,
for instance, envisions himself perfectly executing a complex
dive. Others understand faith as an acceptance of certain religious beliefs or a code of moral practices. Christians, for example, may say they believe in the Ten Commandments and the
teachings of the church. By far, however, a majority view faith
as a tentative suspension of judgment, an attitude of "wait and
see." This kind of faith is highly conditional; it is based on
demands for evidence. It is the faith of Thomas in the gospel
reading of John—"Unless I see in his hands the print of the
nails, and place my finger in the mark of the nails, and place my
hand in his side, I will not believe." Thomas is not a man of
faith; he is a detective seeking proof.

Faith is more than a code of beliefs, a "leap in the dark," or a
suspension of judgment "till all the facts are in." Real faith is the
attitude of a loving heart; it's what makes someone known as a
"faith person." Faith people do not start out with something
specific to believe in, but with a viewpoint of soul. Judgments,
demands for proof, or cynicism are not part of a faith person's
syntax. A loving heart perceives the whole world as full of grace
and wondrous mystery, the creation of a loving God who loves
each of us unconditionally. Love-filled people see other people
as basically good and united with them in the life of the one
same Spirit. If Thomas lived from a perspective of love, of real
faith, when he learned that Jesus had been present in the upper
room, he would have said, "I'm sorry I missed him."

Faith in Jesus as the risen Lord is more than knowing "about"
Jesus: how he looked, what "form" was he in after rising from

41

the dead, how he could be identified by the nail marks in his hands, and so on. Real faith is surrender to God's loving actions manifest in the life and teachings of Jesus. It is a freedom from the need to reason things out, accumulate evidence, and present reasonable proofs. Our challenge as Christians is not to develop more theories "about" Jesus, or to refine theological arguments and proofs of his resurrection, but to develop *ourselves* as people of faith. In the gospel of John, Jesus calls faith people "blessed." They are blessed because they don't have to "see" in order to believe it is loving faith at allows them to really see. As we grow in the spiritual life, we become faith people. As we become more loving, belief becomes second nature to us. Faith, therefore, is basically a way of being.

Consider what it means to be a faith person, rather than a person with a certain set of beliefs. Beliefs come and go; they shift in intensity as we get older and wiser. Real faith is state of soul, a way of life. Pledge yourself to continue your spiritual development. Accept the miracle of the resurrection as perfectly intelligible in light of God's universal and loving care. Accept Jesus as a living Lord who wishes to be part of your life and development. Should miracles enter your life, or be reported to you from others, don't ask for proofs, say rather, "I'm not at all surprised."

TRY SOMETHING DIFFERENT

Part of the gospel reading presents a story of the disciples of Jesus plying their trade as fishermen. As the disciples are offshore in their boats, Jesus calls out to them and asks if they had any luck fishing all night. They confess they didn't. Perhaps the fish weren't running, or the bait was wrong, nevertheless their nets were empty. Jesus suggests they try something different; he tells them to cast their nets on the right side of the boat. When they do so, the nets are filled. We can read a miracle in this story, but we can also learn an important lesson for living more effectively.

Most of us stay in ruts all our lives because of our mind-sets and habits. As creatures of habit, we like things to stay the same. This love of consistency, however, often backfires on us. When the unexpected happens—as it so often does in life—we become distressed and shaken. An accident, for example, can keep us upset for weeks on end. Furthermore, many of us have problems because we ignore the possibility of seeing things differently. We stay in our problems because habit disallows us from trying a different approach. Like a broken walking doll, we continue banging our heads against a wall by trying to resolve our difficulties with solutions that simply don't work.

Society continually finds itself in "crisis" today, not only because new problems keep cropping up, but because, in the face of rapid change, we use formulas that may have been appropriate in other times but no longer serve present needs. We continue to think, for example, that building more jails will solve our problems with crime, that tougher laws will boost the moral tone of the nation, or that raising taxes and more government spending will heal social ills. We often pursue the same

43

nonproductive track in our personal lives. We may persist in a belief that drawing a higher income and acquiring more possessions will bring us happiness. We may believe that belittling a spouse or browbeating children will make them more pliant, or that yelling is the way to prove our convictions. Many of us think we "settle scores" by withholding forgiveness, or can make our problems go away by blaming others.

One encouragement we get from the gospel reading is that we stop lamenting our problems, or beating our heads against the wall, and try to see things in a new light. The lesson in the suggestion of Jesus is that we can often become more effective in meeting our needs simply by trying something different. Maybe learning to smile will prove more productive than demanding our rights. Maybe people would enjoy our company more if we told jokes rather than complained about our ailments. Perhaps hard work can offer more financial promise than pinning our hopes on the lottery. Maybe being more authentic with a spouse or friend, rather than playing mind games, will make for a healthier marriage or a better friendship. Something—anything—different to take us off our dead-end streets.

Do the same problems keep coming up again and again in your life? Is there a pattern in your disappointments with other people? In what area of your life are you fishing on the wrong side of the boat? Try something different. Break your routine, if only for a day, and see what happens. Look at a problem from someone else's point of view. If some expectation of others is constantly causing you conflict, maybe it's illegitimate or misguided. If some habit always brings you grief, maybe it's time to drop it. A solution is not a solution if it doesn't work.

ADULT CHRISTIANITY

One of the most enduring symbols in Christian tradition is Christ the Good Shepherd. The gospel reading recalls this touching image and gives us assurance that Jesus will never abandon his followers. We, the sheep of his flock, are eternally under his guidance and protection. This pledge of care, of course, can be of great comfort to us, especially when we feel like "lost sheep." At the same time, however, we shouldn't let this symbol mislead us. A problem arises when we misconstrue the image of the Good Shepherd and believe it encourages us to remain sheep-like all our lives, especially in terms of our discipleship as Christians. It is one thing to feel confident that we are supported in doing what we are called to do in life, and quite another to go through life dependent on others to take care of us, do our work for us, solve our problems, and make us feel good.

A human being never attains true adulthood until he or she stops being a sheep. All of us desire self-esteem, self-confidence, and respect. But we must realize that these qualities only come at a price. We never develop self-esteem until we own our lives. We can't have self-confidence unless we are in the habit of actually taking care of ourselves. We don't deserve respect unless we take full responsibility for what we do, and for what happens to us. Real maturity and freedom are never enjoyed until we stop being dependent.

The same applies to our Christian faith. Faith cannot empower us as long as it remains only part of a hand-me-down religion; faith has little substance as long as it remains borrowed rather than owned. Being an adult Christian means we take independent responsibility for what we believe, and hold ourselves personally accountable for the way we live out our calling as Christians. It is a good thing, therefore, that our faith is often put to the test. Only when faith is tested does it grow in meaning. Faith becomes a "living faith" when it is challenged and we are put on the line to answer for what we believe. Furthermore, we need to remember that Jesus charged his followers with a mission—one that would entail commitment, hardship, even sacrifice. This isn't sheep talk. Of course we surrender to the will of the Good Shepherd, but his will is that we do our part to help him build the kingdom of God. We are not Christians only so that we can have our religious needs taken care of, but so that we can become engaged in serving the needs of others. The Good Shepherd does not make us dependent, but supports our independence in working for the good of the kingdom wherever we find ourselves.

Do you "own" your faith, or is faith simply something that was passed down to you without much reflection on your part? Do you feel the power of your Christian faith to give you a better quality life? Never fear to have your faith shaken—it will make your faith come alive. Allow your faith to serve you and others. What activities might you get involved in to build the kingdom of God? Are there any parish ministries in which you could become active? Are there ways you can make your home, workplace, or community more enjoyable for everyone? Stop asking, "what am I getting out of this?" and ask rather, "how may I serve?" Fulfill your destiny as a follower of Christ and offer your services in gratitude for all the good things God has done for you.

LOVE IS WHAT LOVE DOES

"A new commandment I give to you, that you love one another . . . By this all men will know that you are my disciples, if you have love for one another." This statement of Jesus, recorded in the gospel reading of John, defines the nature and purpose of Christianity. Jesus makes clear for all time that Christianity is not to be identified with a list of beliefs, a body of doctrines, membership in a particular denomination, or with a particular set of sacred writings, like the Bible. A Christian is fundamentally known by love. For all our religious devotions, loyalty to a particular church, ability to quote Scripture, we cannot legitimately call ourselves "Christian" if we are not committed to being loving persons. The Word of the Lord allows no room here for maneuvering. If the work we do isn't loving, it isn't authentically Christian. If what local congregations teach and preach is not loving, it isn't authentic Christianity. The mark of a Christian is undebatable: Christians are recognized by how much love is reflected in their lives.

But there may be debate about what this love means in practice. Christian churches preach about love all the time, and have done so for centuries. And to what effect? It seems to be an occupational hazard that Christians often confuse, if not substitute, the externals of religion for authentic loving living. A parish, for example, can be a hothouse of social activities, expanding ministries, and magnificent liturgies, and at the same time be a hotbed of competition, infighting, bad will, and prejudice. Furthermore, preaching may never address love in its practical specifics. We may be encouraged to love in general, but never instructed in the art of loving as a Christian. Most of us understand love in romantic or sentimental terms, and get our cues for loving from popular music and television shows. It is easy to be confused about love's meaning. Consequently, we may not know how to give love, receive love, or handle problems with love. We may discover to our chagrin, for example, how difficult it is to maintain a friendship, or share intimacy, or feel God's love for us.

Love nevertheless is what Christianity is all about. It should be obvious that Jesus did not intend to confuse us about his meaning of love. The best way we can understand what the Lord meant by "love" is to observe love as it was modeled by Jesus himself. For Jesus, love was attention given to the needs of others. It was identified with care and service to others in their needs. For Jesus, love meant encouraging others to pursue their spiritual development. It meant helping others find salvation by affirming them and offering them unconditional acceptance and forgiveness. As Christians would be known by their love, that love would be identified in any activity that served the needs of others. Jesus does not view love as a sentimental feeling or as a pious topic for preaching. For Jesus, love is what love *does*.

Make it a daily practice to reflect on the level of your love. Be ready to be challenged on how loving you are. The more "fundamentalist" or "conservative" your position as a Christian, the more your love should be in evidence, because this is what Jesus was fundamentally all about. Don't just talk about the importance of love, put love into practice with members of your family, your neighbors, your work community, even strangers on the street. Love is what love does. How might you be of service to them?

TAKE ADVANTAGE
OF THE SPIRIT

Whatever people's definition of God, there is general consensus that God is a universal Spirit, benevolent, loving, and caring. In the gospel reading, Jesus makes a remarkable revelation about our association with God. He makes it clear that God is not aloof from creation but actually dwells in a loving heart. "If some man loves me , , , we will come to him and make our home with him." Jesus also assures us that God's spirit abides in us as teacher, counselor, and guide. "But the Counselor, the Holy Spirit, whom the Father will send in my name, he will teach you all things." This promise of Jesus is extraordinary good news and should have significant impact for anyone pursuing more effective living. There is immediate comfort in knowing we are never alone, that God is present in us, and for us, at all times. We never need fear that we are isolated in our tribulations, or that we go it alone in our struggles for a better life. But we are further encouraged by the fact that God is actively present in us, prompting and guiding us to higher levels of personal development and quality living.

Most of us don't appreciate, much less utilize, this infinitely powerful resource of God's presence within us. We may claim belief in a universal Spirit that is generally benevolent and concerned for our welfare, but may not be so convinced that we are privileged to be the constant object of immediate divine attention. Which is most unfortunate and much to our loss. It is like suffering in poverty, not knowing that a rich relative has bequeathed us a fortune. With more awareness, however, we might see signs of God operating in our lives. For example, we may be in great sorrow when something totally unexpected comes about to bring us comfort, or we may be in the depths of despair and suddenly be given a glimpse of light. There may be times we receive just the added push we need to accomplish a difficult undertaking, or a golden opportunity presents itself, or a sudden inspiration appears out of nowhere. Luck? Coincidence? Are we not led by the Spirit dwelling within us, often without realizing it? Is it not possible that "coincidence" is merely God's way of remaining anonymous?

We should be encouraged to take advantage of the Spirit's presence within us and actively seek out God's counsel. We can certainly make ourselves more available to God's guidance. God wants us to be happy and to live more effectively. We can ask God for light to set us in the right direction. In the quiet of our hearts we can listen to God prompting us with inspiration to pursue what will best serve our interests. We should never hesitate, therefore, to confer with our indwelling Spirit for whatever help we need to resolve confusions, handle difficult situations, or solve our problems. Jesus assures us that God is not only to be served, but that God wishes to serve us.

Begin each day reflecting on God's presence within you. Work to develop a more active relationship with the Spirit within. Tell God how grateful you are for the help you receive. Ask the Holy Spirit for counsel in your difficulties. Go to God first with your needs, however big or small they may be. Don't be discouraged just because your prayers are not answered according to your designs or timetables—trust that God knows what is in your best interests. Above all, learn to listen. Stop your prayers and quietly listen for a response. Communicate with God, but give God a chance to communicate with you.

ACCEPT AFFIRMATION

Why do we enjoy being fans of sport stars and movie idols? What is it that motivates hero worship and encourages us to stand in long lines to catch a glimpse of our favorites? For some it's fascination with personalities that appear bigger than life. For others it is simply respect for an important model. For most, however, it is a way of living vicariously in the more dramatic, dynamic, and successful lives of others. Heroes and "stars" are adored by millions who have never heard, or trusted, their own call to heroism and stardom.

The call, however, comes to all of us. In our own fashion, each of us is born a destiny that can take us as far as we are willing to venture. There are no inborn limitations to human accomplishment. Every one of us has what it takes to live a life of excellence. What most often prevents us from achieving excellence, however, is not lack of opportunity, but lack of supportive affirmation. Affirmation is a powerful motivation, but many of us have trouble with it. From early life we may have been disaffirmed and taught that we were bad or shameful, that our dreams and ambitions were unrealistic, that our talents were unexceptional. Consequently, we may have stopped dreaming, or we may have difficulty accepting compliments, or we may downplay our accomplishments with disclaimers such as, "oh, it was nothing," or "anybody could have done it." We seem embarrassed by applause because of a misguided belief that we are not deserving.

In the reading from Ephesians, Paul is eloquent in his affirmation of the glorious destiny to which each of us is called. He prays, " . . . that you may know what is the hope to which he has called you, what are the riches of his glorious inheritance in the saints, and what is the immeasurable greatness of his power in us who believe." Can we take a moment to appreciate the significance of this powerful affirmation of us? Can we appreciate the implications this has for our self-esteem? In the gospel reading, Jesus blesses his disciples as he departs from them. Reminding them of their great mission to be his witnesses, he tells them, "I send the promise of my Father upon you." But *we* are disciples of Jesus; *we* have his promise and blessing. We are destined to perform great things in witness of his love.

Arrogance is not a problem for most people, lack of healthy pride is. One of the most important steps we can take to live more effectively is to learn to accept affirmations. There is a hero and "star" in each of us that needs acclamation, honor, and respect. We should never discount our dreams or downplay our accomplishments. Jesus exhorts us not to hide our light under a bushel basket. We are called to glory and have nothing to be ashamed of. The good that we do far outweighs the bad, and what we have done is as nothing compared to great things we have yet to accomplish. In our work, in our relationships, in our ministries in the church, in our spiritual development, "the sky is the limit."

What great things still await you in life? Don't give up on your dreams. Never put yourself down, or allow others to do so. Respond to compliments with, "thank you," rather than a disclaimer. Learn to affirm yourself more. Pat yourself on the back when you've achieved a goal you set for yourself. Take pride in your achievements. God does not make mistakes. You were born for stardom.

STAY CONNECTED

One of the most enduring images of American folklore is the cowboy hero riding off into the sunset—all alone. Our culture promotes an ideal of rugged individualism. One of the greatest marks of achievement in our socety is to be dependent on no one. Few people in the business world command more respect than the "self-made" man or woman. Of course there is something admirable about being independent and self-reliant, but an attitude of going it alone can also lead to isolation and a loss of joy that comes from intimate and supportive relationships. It is hardly flattering, for example, that the cowboy hero has a horse for a best friend. We can't ignore the fact that we are social animals. We cannot escape our dependence upon one another, not only for the necessities we need to survive, but for our personal development as well. Happy and effective living is impossible without graceful interactions with other people. Feeling lonely is painful, but it is nature's way of telling us that something is wrong with our situation and that we should be relating to others better than we are. We are born to love and be loved in an ever widening web of relationships.

The gospel reading amplifies this truth beautifully. Jesus prays for his followers in a manner that allows no ambiguity to his meaning. "That they may be one even as we are one, I in them and thou in me, that they may become perfectly one." Christianity is a community religion. Nowhere in the teachings of Jesus is "rugged individualism" promoted as an option for Christian spirituality. Christians would be known by their love and interconnectedness in caring relationships. The gospel passage reads almost like a poem of ecstasy as Jesus refers to God living in us and we living in God, and all of us living in one another. When we live in one another, we not only share one another's burdens, we share one another's blessings, strengths, and joys as well. One of the major blessings of healthy relationships is that the success of one becomes the good fortune of all.

Our personal development and spiritual growth need to be built on a foundation of mutually supportive relationships. Effective people network. Service toward all members is the hallmark of a thriving parish community. Support groups all across the nation demonstrate the empowerment that comes from a community spirit. Can anyone deny the extraordinary blessing found in a loving family and intimate friendships? Furthermore, can we appreciate that most of the problems we face in life are relational problems? The emotional pain we suffer most frequently arises from our inability to relate and communicate effectively. Our difficulties often stem from beliefs we've grown up with that we are separate, that other people are threats to our security, and that our needs are unconnected with the needs of others. We need to be mindful, therefore, of the importance of being connected. One of our primary concerns should be for "us."

What is your ideal for a happy life? Do you believe people are happier by interacting, or by being left alone? Try to see the advantages of working with others, over and above what you can do on your own. Stay connected. Nurture your relationships and look for opportunities to network. Let people know how much they mean to you, especially members of your family and your friends. Be there for others as you would appreciate them being there for you. Notice how your needs are often best served by helping others.

LIVING WITH PASSION

The reading from Acts speaks of rushing wind, fire, and Spirit that brought a group of frightened disciples out of hiding and energized them to go out and conquer the world for Christ. They were filled with enthusiasm, and all who witnessed it were amazed. The events in this reading probably stand out in sharp contrast to how we normally experience life, and especially our mission to be witnesses of Christ and his message. It is easy for life to become humdrum, if not discouraging. The never-ending responsibilities and ordeals we routinely face every day have a way of draining our ambition. Yes, we do what we have to do, but very often our heart isn't in it. We work at our job and tend to our obligations, but do so with less and less enthusiasm. Even prayer and worship become dry. Sometimes it strikes us that we should be doing more with our lives, but the feeling doesn't last. Over time we become more resigned to life than excited about future prospects.

In his letter to the Corinthians, Paul says, "Now there are varieties of gifts, but the same Spirit." What we need to understand here is that we share the Spirit that flooded the apostles with energy and enthusiasm. The Spirit is the same, and is always with us. Our personal development is never complete. We have work to do to build ourselves and the kingdom of God, and the Spirit continually urges us onto new heights. The work of the Spirit, however, can be significantly thwarted by our proclivities toward laziness, apathy, and resignation. As we get older, we tend to stop setting goals; we back down from commitments and run away from challenges; we're reluctant to try something new. If we wish a better quality life, however, we need to fight these tendencies. The Spirit is always present to us as energy, but it is up to us to tap into that energy by struggling against the forces of gravity that would pull us down. What this means is that we make a conscious choice for growth rather than comfort, for risk rather than safety, for more life rather than slow death.

Christians are Pentecost people, people with "spirit." We stay "alive," and feel most alive, when we determine to live with passion. We all know what a potent force enthusiasm can be. As a good coach might revive his dispirited team at half-time, it is up to us to rally ourselves to new zest in our marriage, better performance in our job, new friends, new interests, new activities, and new heights for our spiritual growth. We raise our spirits by living with spirit in everything we do.

> As you think, so you are. What kind of thoughts occupy your mind most of the day? Dark, depressing thoughts, or positive, energizing thoughts? How you feel is up to you, by the kind of thoughts you allow. Wake up seeing every new day as full of possibilities for your happiness. Remember, it's your attitude that sets the tone for what you will experience. Take responsibility for your energy levels. Read books that inspire you. Avoid people who make you feel down and associate more with people who build you up. Make sure you eat properly and make regular exercise part of your daily routine. Commit yourself to live with passion and your spirits will rise.

THE WONDER OF GOD

The solemnity of the Holy Trinity celebrates the mystery of God the Father, Son, and Holy Spirit: three persons in one God. A long history of complex theological debate has tried to explain how this can be. But we know there is no "explaining" a mystery; mysteries can only arouse our awe. Our encouragement today, therefore, is not to try to make sense of the Trinity, but to peacefully contemplate the wonder of God. If God is God, we also need to review our relationship with the very source of our life and being. Furthermore, we need to challenge our ideas about God, and evaluate how well we are fulfilling the destiny for which our creator has designed us.

What an awesome thing it is to contemplate God! What a tribute to our spiritual natures that we are able to ponder God without being crushed by the awesomeness of it all. Moreover, to accept, as Paul reminds the Romans, that "God's love has been poured into our hearts through the Holy Spirit who has been given to us," is a wonder beyond all imagination. To dwell on God and God's love for us is one of the most effective ways of enhancing our lives. We cannot truly believe in that love without feeling eminently safe and cared for, and without being moved to become the best that we can be.

Our relationship to God should be our life's primary concern, and feeling close to God our greatest joy. God's love is never neutral, it attracts and beckons us at all times. We are designed to be united with God. Isn't that the reason, for example, that no matter how much success we achieve, no matter what our accomplishments in life, or how vast our possessions, we are never completely satisfied? Can we appreciate that our chronic dissatisfactions are simply an indication of a fulfillment that only God can supply?

It is also important that we challenge our ideas about God. What we think about God will significantly affect the way we relate to God. Some of us may perceive God as aloof and distant, or as a fearsome judge of our moral failings. On the other hand, some of us may believe that God has little care for how we direct and run our lives. All these perceptions of God are questionable in light of the teachings of Jesus. Jesus was unambiguous that God dwells within us and is an unconditional font of love and forgiveness. Jesus was also clear that God has designs for creation, and has definite expectations of us. Our growth as spiritual beings is not simply to survive this life, avoid sin, and conduct our religious practices, but to develop ourselves according to God's purpose for us, revealed in Christ. That purpose, according to Jesus, is to become as loving as we can.

Set time aside today to think about God. Let your joy run over that God is, and that God cares for you with unmeasurable love. Pray to the Spirit dwelling in your heart. Express gratitude for God's presence. Acknowledge your longings for the infinite and also express thanks to the Spirit for drawing you closer to God. Ask the Spirit further to help you align your goals in life with the purpose God has for you. As a Christian, be committed to revealing the presence of God within you by pouring your love out to others. This is the best way to praise the Father, Son, and Holy Spirit.

LIVE FROM
YOUR STRENGTHS

One of the splendors of creation is the extraordinary variety of life. Every form of life has its unique role to play in God's plan. The great oaks, for example, daffodils, elephants, canaries, dolphins, and sharks each have their own design and purpose. They achieve their destinies by being just what they are, and functioning according to the nature of their species. Human beings, however, go one step better. We differ from plants and animals, not only because we are of a different species, but because each one of us is unique—almost an individual species in ourself. There is nobody else in the world exactly like us, nor has there ever been, nor will there ever be. It follows, therefore, that we will achieve our destiny by being just what we are, and functioning according to our uniqueness.

One of the most important steps we make in living effectively is to understand and respect our uniqueness. Each of us has our own life to unfold and our own destiny to accomplish. God has a plan, specific for each of us as individuals, to manifest God's glory, and our own. But accepting our uniqueness, with all that it implies, is not easy. Many people don't like themselves. Millions are not happy with who they are or what they have. It is unfortunate that many of us spend our lives wallowing in envy of others. Rather than accomplishing our own purposes, we waste time and energy complaining about our supposed deficiencies, and wishing we had someone else's looks, personalities, talents, social advantages, and financial means.

All that we need to be happy and fulfilled in life we already have. In his powerful letter to the Corinthians, Paul makes it clear that each of us possesses unique talents and gifts. No one has exactly the same endowments and we have no right to expect it to be otherwise. While we are all inspired by one, same Spirit, that Spirit manifests itself through the distinctiveness of our individuality. Someone, for example, may "speak in tongues," but it may take someone else to interpret what is being said. As Paul alludes, the common good, and our own good, is served not by everybody trying to be the same, or by everyone wishing to be someone else, but by being true to our individual natures, temperaments, and gifts. We achieve our purpose in life by discovering, and living from, our own strengths.

We must stop looking outside ourselves, therefore, for reasons to be happy and successful. All that we need is already within. Each of us must discover what we have to offer to leave our mark on this world. Perhaps it is to be a remarkable parent, a fine musician, an exceptional handyman, a devoted teacher, a wise counselor, an honest politician, a model of longsuffering. We can only work from what we *have*, not from what we feel we're missing. Furthermore, we need to keep in mind that God doesn't make comparisons and neither should we. In God's eyes, no one is more appealing, more talented, more beautiful, or more perfect. When we are unique, we are already perfect; because there really is no one else like us, there is no need for comparisons. We need to see, therefore, as God sees. We work to achieve our own excellence, in our own unique way.

Do you find yourself talking more about what you're missing in life than about what you have? Do you often find yourself envious of other people? Can you appreciate how it prevents you from living your own life? Stop comparing yourself with others. Look at yourself first and what you have to offer. Accept who you are and what you have. Your potential is infinite as long as you work with your uniqueness. Focus on your strengths.

Nehemiah 8:1–4a, 5–6, 8–10 **1 Corinthians 12: 12–30**
Luke 1:1–4, 4:14–21

WE ARE ONE

Few societies are as consumed with promoting and protecting the rights of individuals as our own. In the last half century or so, the individual has assumed paramount status. Looking out for "Number One" has become a moral imperative for millions, and "what's in it for me?" an exclusive concern. We generally accept the premises of "leave me alone," "don't bother me and I won't bother you," and "if you step on me, you will live to regret it." The consequences are obvious. Lawsuits have become one of the biggest industries in the land. Social stratification, the worship of private property, and fierce economic competition bordering on thievery, divide us, as does suspicion, and an unprecedented level of mistrust. While diligent care of one's personal well-being is certainly a reasonable objective for any individual, self-love has often degenerated into a self-centeredness that is exacting a terrible toll on whole segments of society that are lonely, alienated, and fixated in narcissistic addictions.

Paul, in his letter to the Corinthians, is well aware of the dangers of exaggerated individualism, especially among Christian believers. Paul is a passionate promoter of the unity of the body of Christ and knows how easily that unity can be fragmented. He fully acknowledges our individuality—"For the body does not consist of one member but of many"—but emphatically reminds us that we are members of one body, sharing "one Spirit." What Paul is encouraging here is an attitude that respects the whole as well as the parts. Individualism has its limits. We may be different, with different gifts and destinies to pursue, but we are one. Just as our body has many parts, each functioning according to its design, it is still one body. Should part of the body go off on its own, as is the case with cancer, for example, the whole body suffers.

Spiritual masters of all times, and conservationists in our

own, have been great promoters of "unity consciousness," that we be aware of how connected we are. Science demonstrates that everything in the universe, from the tiniest of atoms to the largest of galaxies, exists in a dynamic relationship. It is important, therefore, for our spiritual development, and for the well-being of society, that we appreciate that we are never alone, working exclusively on our own agendas with only ourselves in mind, and that we maintain a vision of the whole of which we are a part. We have a responsibility, not only to ourselves, but to the whole body of mankind. We are our brother's keeper; society's problems are our problems; global issues are our issues. If and when the whole functions better, we ourselves benefit. As Paul notes, "If one member suffers, all suffer together; if one member is honored, all rejoice together." We each reap the benefits only if we are all united.

Can you appreciate individual rights but, at the same time, the importance of the common good? What do you do to foster the well-being of any group or relationship of which you are a part? Do you find it easy to make personal sacrifices for the welfare and happiness of others? Take care of yourself and your needs, but never at another's expense. Contribute what you can to make your home, workplace, or parish a happy place for everyone. Be aware that everything you do has repercussions on someone else. Reflect how others may be affected by your decisions and actions. Better, find opportunities to spread your love.

TEST OF ADULTHOOD

"Adulthood" can be defined in different ways. Society grants adult status to an individual at eighteen or twenty-one years of age. Becoming "legal" allows many young people to believe that they have "arrived." Most of us perceive adulthood as a watershed in life where we begin to consider ourselves "grown up." We measure adulthood with the ability to think more for ourselves, with being more independent, and with being legally responsible for our actions. Adulthood is also associated with more stable living, control of impulses, and more objectivity in seeing things as they are. Paul makes a point of this in his letter to the Corinthians, when he says: "When I was a child, I spoke like a child, I thought like a child, I reasoned like a child; when I became a man, I gave up childish ways."

The assumption that we really do put away childish ways when we grow up should not be made too quickly, however. Legal age, we know, is a poor determinant of adulthood. Many people never grow up; they maintain childish ways for a lifetime. An infant's whining over toys, for example, is not abandoned, only upgraded to more sophisticated complaining. We may find that our relationships are a constant source of stress because we handle them as a petulant child might. The stubbornness we exhibited as children may just evolve into our being "set in our ways." Too much being taken care of by mommy can easily slip into an adult expectation to be taken care of by a spouse, one's family, or the government. Even the wild impulses of youth may not be forsaken, they are simply galvanized in addictions of one kind or another. And, as for being more objective and logical, we might observe, in the gospel passage from Luke, how "adult" Jesus' audience was acting in wanting to throw him off a cliff for remarks he made in a sermon.

It is obvious in the letter to the Corinthians that Paul draws a close connection between love and being an adult. As a matter of fact, one of the best measurements we can take of how adult we have become—and of how much we have given up our childish ways—is to examine our love. Nowhere is adult love better described than by Paul: "Love is patient and kind; love is not jealous or boastful; it is not arrogant or rude. Love does not insist on its own way; it is not irritable or resentful; it does not rejoice at wrong, but rejoices in the right. Love bears all things, believes all things, hopes all things, endures all things." This is quite an earful for reflection, and a wonderful opportunity for us to measure how much into adulthood we are.

Can you spot "childish ways" that still control aspects of your life? Do you take ownership of your life and actions, or is your life basically a reaction to what other people say and do? The gospel tells us that Jesus simply walked away from those who misunderstood him. Do you simply walk away from fruitless arguments and disagreements, or do you feel pressed to prove other people wrong and that you are right? Is your temper often out of control; do you still engage in tantrums? Do you complain more about what you don't have rather than show gratitude for what you do have? Are you concerned more about getting than giving? Commit yourself to adult living. Demonstrate your maturity in attitudes and behavior that flow from the love Paul so eloquently describes.

LEAVE IT BEHIND

Most of us would love a better and happier life. We wish we could be more effective in handling our feelings, careers, relationships, and problems. We don't often realize, however, that what holds us back is not lack of opportunity for making a better life for ourselves, but the hundreds of little anchors that prevent us from sailing into more promising waters. Life becomes a "drag" because we drag around so much baggage. We don't enjoy the trip because we are always worrying about the luggage! Many of us are prevented from seeing golden opportunities for improvement because we're so distracted with petty preoccupations. Or, when opportunities do arise, we don't take advantage of them because we immediately start focusing on our shortcomings. We sometimes enjoy the good things we have, but, as certain as the sun rises in the morning, we regress to thinking about what we don't have. At times we become inspired to improve our situation, but then we hinder any progress we might make with unworkable beliefs and the same old ways of looking at things.

In the gospel reading from Luke, we see Jesus inviting his future apostles to a higher way of life. Jesus tells these fishermen that, "henceforth you will be catching men." Whatever moved them, the narrative ends with the invitation being accepted. At a price! If they wanted to follow Jesus into a new life, the disciples had to leave their boats behind. And this should come as no surprise. It is impossible to move on to bigger and better things for ourselves without leaving something behind. There comes a time when the "baggage" simply has to go. A student, for example, who becomes serious about getting better grades will likely have to give up more fun and free time. A rising executive who is offered a promotion may have to move from established surroundings to a new location. A client who hopes for success in therapy will be required to abandon some favorite, but self-destructive, mind-sets. Every change, every improvement for ourselves, will involve necessary losses.

Life has no greater wish than to endow us with its favors, but also demands that we give up certain things to possess them. If we want the freedom of an uncluttered life, we may need to dispossess ourselves of some of our belongings. If we want better health, we may need to forsake poor eating habits, lack of exercise, and abusive addictions. If we want peace of mind, we will have to give up resorting to argumentativeness and demands that other people see things our way. If we want to improve our minds, we may have to turn off the television. If we want to climb mountains, we have to leave our fishing boats on the shore. That's life! Everything good has its price. As much as an old way of life may have its redeeming qualities, if we desire major improvements, it means we will have to muster the courage to give it up.

Recognize the "baggage" that holds you back from effective living. Make a list of what you really need in life to make you happy, and what you don't. What is holding you back from having a better quality life? Are your attitudes and expectations misguided? Do you believe, for example, that your options in life are limited, or that members of your family exist to take care of you, or that your spouse has to be perfect? Are you so choked with business concerns, making money, outwitting your competitors, that you still haven't found the time to smell the roses? Check your "luggage"—what can you leave behind?

BLESSINGS IN DISGUISE

The gospel reading presents a sermon of Jesus that won't get much of a sympathetic hearing from anyone brought up with the imagery of the American Dream. Jesus offers for our consideration the beatitudes: what it takes to find "beatitude," or happiness, in life. For us, being poor, hungry, or an object of scorn, would hardly merit admiration, much less willing acceptance of these human miseries. Implying, for instance, that we are "blessed" in our weeping seems outrageous. And yet, this is exactly what Jesus seems to be doing. At first glance, we may believe that Jesus is offering a very pessimistic life view, or that he is encouraging resignation to misfortune. But, from what we know from many other teachings of Jesus, these couldn't be his intentions. Jesus announced his mission with a promise of happiness. "I have come that you may have joy, and that your joy may be complete." He proclaimed he was "the way, the truth, and the life." Jesus came to offer life, and life in abundance.

Hunger and poverty can only be considered "blessed" if we understand something important about human motivation. Jesus promises us abundant life but leaves no doubt that, to attain it, we have to make some significant changes in our attitudes and behavior. But what is it that actually motivates us to change? Poverty, hunger, scorn, and sadness are not blessings in themselves, but can certainly be seen as blessings in *disguise*. Rarely do we change anything about ourselves until our discomfort rises to unacceptable levels. Most people, for example, don't seek medical attention until an illness is already taking its toll. Most alcoholics don't begin recovering from the grips of their addiction until they hit the "bottom of the barrel." Until a divorce is imminent, most people in a dysfunctional marriage won't seek counseling. Pain is a call to action; often nothing substitutes for it. Suffering can push us to take care of ourselves like nothing else can.

Rather than resign ourselves to our troubles, therefore, or complain about our hardships, we need to take a proactive approach toward whatever afflicts us. Whatever it is, there is a blessing in disguise, a lesson, in every suffering we endure. There is something we are meant to learn or do for our betterment. Pain, mental or physical, tells us in no uncertain terms that something has to change. A "problem" informs us that an attitude or approach we are using with certain people or situations isn't working, and that we need to try something different. Suffering motivates us to take corrective action. That is precisely what makes any affliction "blessed." Without "hunger," for example, for a better life, our spiritual development would never advance.

See the beatitudes in terms of motivation—you can't be "satisfied" unless you hunger. Can you accept, therefore, that your sufferings, hardships, and problems may be blessings in disguise? Consider, in retrospect, how many times you suffered in the past—"for no reason"—only to discover later that something good came out of it. Trust that nothing happens to you in this world without some reason in God's loving plan. Learn something from any affliction you bear. Ask yourself: "What is this loneliness, this depression, this anger, this heartache, this illness, this misfortune trying to teach me?" "Why am I fearful all the time, or tired, or cranky, or hypercritical of others?" "What do I need to change?" Blessed are they who try to learn from their afflictions, for they will be enlightened.

SEVENTH SUNDAY IN ORDINARY TIME
1 Samuel 26:2, 7–9, 12–13,22–23 1 Corinthians 15:45–49 **Luke 6:27–38**

THE HEART
HAS ITS REASONS

Perhaps no other passage in the gospels better presents an over-all perspective of the teachings of Jesus than today's reading from Luke. And there is perhaps no other passage more at odds with our customary ways of handling other people. One sentence after another pounds us with an instruction that goes against the grain of what we have long come to feel and believe. "Love your enemies, do good to those who hate you, bless those who curse you, pray for those who abuse you." "Judge not …condemn not…forgive." Who can live these teachings? Can you imagine what our enemies would do to us if we didn't fight them? Doesn't experience demonstrate that, if you "turn the other cheek," people will likely hit you there too? Isn't it true that once you start giving to beggars they become more dependent? If we love people with no expectations of them, isn't that giving them a green light to take advantage of us? And when it comes to not judging people, where would society be if we didn't have our courts and prisons?

We could argue with Jesus on every one of his proposals, and we could do so reasonably in the light of logic and common sense. Nothing Jesus proposes in this gospel narrative makes sense. But here we approach a pivotal understanding of Christianity. Christianity is basically a love religion, and, as any of us who has ever been in love knows, there isn't much logic, or even common sense, in real love. Love has its own rules, its own logic, its own evaluations, its own way of dealing with others. Once we become truly loving, we begin to see things in a whole new light. In short, the heart has its reasons.

Jesus is not proposing impossible expectations of his followers; he is simply presenting a variety of examples of what loving people do *naturally*. If we happen to know genuinely loving people, we know this is true. We may notice they don't have "enemies." They usually make excuses for someone's bad behavior and try to point out some redeeming quality in the worst of offenders. Loving people are normally known for being "a soft touch"; we might say of someone: "he'd give you the shirt off his back." Loving people live by different standards. They truly believe, for example, "there is more joy in giving than receiving," and find it easy to express their love without expecting something in return. When we are most authentically Christian, when we love authentically, something happens deep inside us: our perceptions change dramatically; the world and other people simply look different; "condemn not" becomes second nature to us. To a loving person, everything Jesus proposes in this passage makes perfect sense.

Does this gospel narrative move you, or threaten you? Do you find yourself immediately coming up with solid reasons to show that, practically speaking, there have to be exceptions and conditions to the ideals Jesus sets forth? How flexible is your heart? What do you think it means to be a "good" Christian? Consider the level of your love. Don't expect overnight changes without a special grace, but you can take small steps to melt any hardness of heart by doing exactly what Jesus prescribes. Say a prayer for someone who dislikes you. Go out of your way to help a stranger. Say, "don't worry about it," to someone who borrows from you. Stop judging other people and forgive at the drop of a hat. Live with the reasons of your heart.

IF THE SHOE FITS

"Why do you see the speck that is in your brother's eye, but do not notice the log that is in your own eye?" This observation by Jesus in the reading from Luke offers us an important lesson about criticizing others. We are definitely two-faced when we put down other people for the very faults we have ourselves. While we may protest strongly that we are being "objective," there is something hypocritical, for example, about engaging in gossip about other gossips, or in complaining about petty theft in the office when we routinely pad our expense accounts. Furthermore, there is great validity in the popular saying, "It takes one to know one." This wisdom is confirmed by psychologists who note that the failings a client tends to see in others are generally the client's own. This tendency is called "projection." When we become upset, for instance, that someone has not fulfilled a promise, it may be that we regularly renege on our promises. When we become angry with another's immaturity, we are likely burdened with our own. If it bothers us that a friend is inconsiderate or selfish, it is more than likely that our own selfishness is being triggered by what he or she does.

Seen from another angle, therefore, there is something positive we can get from Jesus' censure of hypocrisy and criticism. Understanding how projection works, we can learn a lot about *ourselves* through our judgments of others. Self-knowledge is very important to effective living and spiritual growth. It's to our benefit if we can accept criticism from others, and learn from it, without immediately going on the defensive and attacking our critics. But it is also of great benefit to our development if we can look upon our judgments of others as indicative of something *we* need to work on in *ourselves*. In short, criticizing others has merit as long as we are committed to see if the shoe fits us first. For example, what is it that bothers us most about a spouse, parent, or coworker? Notice the word "bothers." Being "bothered" is something different from making a calm, cool, clinical assessment of a fact. When we are "disturbed," something is being triggered in us. We need to look at that, and come to terms with why we feel "offended" in the first place. Why do we get "upset," for example, when a reservation we made at a restaurant is not immediately honored? Is it possible that we are being subtly reminded of commitments we don't keep? Why do we get angry at a teenager's laziness, or someone talking too much? Could it be that our own laziness is being exposed, or that we want to monopolize a conversation in our own way? Again, the fact that we are "bothered" tells us something more about *ourselves* than about another person. Jesus, therefore, makes an important point: criticisms we make of others are some of the best stepping-stones to self-knowledge and growth.

> Check yourself out by catching on to your judgments of others. Ask yourself: "What kind of projection is going on here?" What faults are you continually noticing in people around you? What habitually annoys you about the people you work with? Is it stubbornness, negativity, lack of initiative and drive, and could these possibly be reflecting some of your own weaknesses? Do you get upset easily when others are not on time, or are lacking in focus, or are halfhearted in their endeavors? What causes your blood pressure to rise, or embarrasses you about the antics of young people? Are you not perhaps looking into a mirror? Take your criticisms seriously, therefore. They have a lot to teach you about yourself—if you are open enough to learn. Does the shoe fit?

BROADEN YOUR HORIZONS

Most of us were brought up with certain beliefs about what it takes to get through life successfully. From parents, relatives, and teachers alike we might have heard: "mind your own business," "don't stick your neck out," "stay in your own backyard," and "don't get involved." These formulas certainly appeal to our survival instincts and may keep us relatively safe on the road of life, but they also insure a life's journey that will be isolated, impoverished, and dull. Millions of people don't "go" anywhere in life because they misguidedly restrict their horizons.

Which is exactly what the gospel today confronts. The reading from Luke challenges our inclination to keep our concerns "private." Jesus is presented reaching out to a centurion who was a gentile, an unbeliever, an officer of the hated Roman army that was occupying Palestine. The miracle Jesus offered was more than a simple return of a favor for the centurion's generosity to the local synagogue. Rather, it was a testimony of the open-endedness of the Christian perspective. When Jesus commissioned his apostles to preach the good news, he told them to go out to "all the world." Christian love was not to be "private," or restricted to boundaries. The whole world is our "backyard," and everybody is our "business."

Can we appreciate how enriched life becomes when we broaden the horizons of our minds and hearts? We are not born to stay in our own backyards, but to participate in a bigger drama. And, if we are willing to risk leaving the protective borders we put up around our little worlds, we make some important discoveries. It is encouraging, for example, to learn that our problems are far from unique and are shared by millions who struggle with the same issues. Developing concern for the problems of society puts our own problems into perspective, and allows them to appear less catastrophic. A dispute with a coworker, for instance, doesn't seem as monumental when we feel compassion for the conflicts that split whole nations. Furthermore, can we pretend that society's problems, or even the problems of our neighbors, don't affect us sooner or later? Will the deterioration of the inner city, for example, not eventually take its toll on the comforts and security of suburban living? Caring for others is often the best way to care for ourselves.

The gospels continually urge us to widen our perspectives and broaden our horizons. Spiritual growth is stretching our identities and enlarging our capacities to know and to love. An enriched life is one that is continually expanding to incorporate an ever-widening community. Our interests and concerns need to go beyond our private worlds. This was clearly evident in the example of Jesus, but also evident in the centurion who trusted that Jesus could cure his servant from a distance. The centurion had a faith that helped him escape the narrow-mindedness of a non-Jewish military official of an occupying force—and Jesus marveled at it.

What perspective governs your life? Are you a citizen of the world or are you privatized in your own world of fear, mistrust, and general apathy about the needs of others? Do you believe that the only purpose of life is to survive? Stretch yourself. Broaden your horizons. Expand your knowledge and compassion. Look upon other people as "us" instead of "them." Get involved with your parish and your community; volunteer your services to make this world a little better place for everyone. You grow as your horizons expand.

DEATH BRINGS
APPRECIATION OF LIFE

Once upon a time there were two very close friends, Ron and Rich, who had a passion for playing baseball. They always wondered if there was baseball in heaven and made a promise to each other that whoever died first would come back and tell the other if there was. Ron died and went to heaven, and some weeks later Rich was walking home from work when, all of a sudden, he heard Ron's unmistakable voice. "I've got good news, and bad news, Rich," he said. "The good news is that there is baseball in heaven; the bad news is that there's a big game coming up next Friday, and you're pitching."

It's good that we can tell jokes about death, but death itself is not easy to laugh at. The widow of Naim in the gospel narrative is heartbroken and distraught over the death of her son. Death is never kind, and when we are confronted with death we tend to ask soul-wrenching questions. Why? Why this way? Why this person? Why now? And people respond in a variety of ways. Some turn away and don't want to talk about it. Some get angry with God, or even the deceased. Some, with cynical resignation, say: "that's the breaks." Others express relief that the dead person's sufferings are over.

Christians, however, trusting in a resurrected Lord, have an unabashed belief that life is stronger than death. We profess that a God who can give life once, can certainly give it again—and does. Jesus says to the dead man in the gospel: "Young man, I say to you, arise," and the young man sits up and speaks. We can rejoice with the mother who gets back her only son but we should also rejoice over something deeper: life itself. Jesus proclaimed that his mission was to bring us life in abundance. If we believe in a living God, we should not only ask serious questions about death, we should also ask serious questions about life, our own life specifically. If life is stronger than death, our lives should reflect this belief in everything we do. Reflecting on our deaths should not depress us, but should energize us to become more invested in living to the fullest. Thoughts of death, therefore, can sharpen our sensitivity and give us a better appreciation of life. Nature, for example, is seen more in her splendor; sunsets become more magnificent. The touch of a spouse's hand becomes more significant. Relationships become more important; conversations with friends become more meaningful and endearing. Simple things take on grandeur. A sparrow's twitter begins to rival the music of Mozart; a glass of cool water tastes like wine. If we believe in the power of life, we should engage in it with more mindfulness. We can raise ourselves from the dead by becoming more aware of the wonder of life.

Think about death for a moment. Do you fear dying because you haven't lived enough yet? If you were assured this was to be the last year of your life, what would you set out to accomplish? What dreams in you are still unfulfilled? Are you genuinely happy to be alive? Is this reflected in the way you live? Do you engage in life-enhancing practices of seeing hope, the vastness of your potential, your assets, the beauty of the natural world, the good side of things, the goodness in people? Stop wasting valuable life on things that don't matter. Commit yourself to develop your life to the fullest. Remember that, in the end, only the spirit of your love will live on forever. Invest in loving living.

NOTHING NEUTRAL

From the beginning, the Church has understood that Jesus left us a living memorial of himself in the sacramental presence of his body and blood. The gospel narrative of Luke presents the miracle of Jesus multiplying loaves of bread as a foreshadowing of the miracle of the Eucharist. Paul's letter to the Corinthians recalls the Last Supper when Jesus broke bread with his disciples and assured them, "This is my body which is for you." The presence of the living Christ under the forms of bread and wine is a great mystery. But the mystery is by no means unacceptable when we take into account Jesus' unmeasurable love for us. When he offers himself as our food and drink, he expresses love at its most intimate. Jesus wishes to be part of our very being, living in us soul and body. As the food we eat becomes part of our life, the Eucharist brings Christ's own life into our own.

The gift of Christ sharing his life with us should encourage us to reflect on how much we bring life to others. Jesus announced that his purpose was to bring abundant life to those who would accept him. Our purpose as Christians is the same. We can better understand our purpose if we appreciate something significant about our behavior. Nothing we do is ever neutral. Every action we perform has consequences. Everything we do in our interactions with other people has an effect. We either bring life, or we bring forms of death. When we come into work, for example, a cheerful "good morning" can set a positive tone for the whole day for our coworkers. Praise for some small task done by our children can motivate them to live productively. A two-minute call to one's mother can brighten her week. Holding the door open for a stranger in a shopping mall can turn a cynic's snarl into a smile of gratitude. On the other hand, an offhand remark can spoil a spouse's otherwise happy morning. A display of temper can make a small child feel unloved. A criticism can harden a neighbor's already unfriendly attitude. If we think about it, nothing we do is without its effect; we either lift up or we put down.

In his teachings, his compassion, his acts of healing, his wise counsel, his assurances of love, Jesus brought life into the lives of the people he touched. This is our goal. A small stone thrown into the water will send ripples across an entire lake. We need to be sensitive to how our behavior affects others and commit ourselves to never bring harm to anyone. Following the example of Jesus, we should look forward every day to how we can increase life in the people whose lives we touch, and beyond. If our hearts are set on sharing our love and making others happy, we are on the right track.

Let the miracle of the Eucharist encourage your own miracle making. Every morning, make a choice to be a life-giver for that day. Say to yourself: "I have come to bring life in abundance to others." Look at each member of your family and decide how you might bring them a better life. Do you need to be more understanding and compassionate? Do you need to offer more praise and affirmation? Tell the people you love how much you care for them. Be more observant of the things you do all day long and notice the effect your actions have on others. Vow to never hurt anyone. Rather, share your life as Christ shares life with you.

Love and the Law

Where would civilization be without laws? How could society function without law and order? Most of us believe we need more laws, and stricter enforcement of laws, if we ever hope to resolve the chronic ills afflicting society. Many of us are convinced that family life prospers when all family members adhere to established house rules. Without question, law is important for the well-being of society. But we need to understand something important about law. Law basically concerns itself with restrictions; it tells us what we shouldn't do. The purpose of law is to protect rather than to empower; it doesn't so much make good things happen as prevent something bad from happening. In other words, law safeguards life, but does not of itself nurture it. When we depend on the law, therefore, to raise the moral tone of society, or to enrich our life, we are asking for something it simply cannot provide.

Paul, in the reading from Galatians, is essentially aware of this. He declares how futile law and law-keeping are to make us feel justified. Our only hope for justification is through faith in Jesus Christ. The law does not bring life. For Paul, the only life worth living comes from the life of Christ: "it is no longer I who live, but Christ who lives in me." Paul, of course, is not saying law has no place in society, or in our lives, but that it is woefully insufficient to bring us the kind of life we were made for. Where law is concerned with judgments and punishments, it is love that increases life's abundance. If we were more concerned about love, we wouldn't need to worry so much about the law. By the same token, Paul would caution us not to become smug in thinking our life is fulfilled, or all that it should be, because we are "law-abiding citizens." Without love, life is empty, no matter how scrupulously we obey every rule and regulation.

In the gospel reading from Luke, Jesus carries this concept even further. He is anointed with perfumed oil by a woman we presume to be a prostitute. She is considered a public sinner, and Jesus' host at dinner is obviously annoyed that Jesus doesn't rightfully recognize her as an object of scorn. Jesus pronounces, however, that this woman's many sins (breaking of the law) are easily forgiven, because "she loved much." What Jesus is saying is that love covers a multitude of sins. This should give us a great sense of relief. We are not given a license to sin, but, as long as we are trying to be loving persons, we can be assured that God considers our sins pardoned. There is no need, therefore, to burden ourselves with guilt trips, and no reason to look down on ourselves for mistakes of the past. Love sets us free from our failings so we can continue our spiritual journey with a lighter spirit.

Are you more concerned about being a law-abiding citizen than a loving person? In your estimation, have all the laws passed by government in the last few decades improved the common good, brought down the crime rate, or given most people a greater sense of security? On the other hand, have you ever witnessed the miracles of change brought about by loving people? Give love a chance to show you its miraculous powers. In place of multiplying house rules, what can you do to increase love in your home? Try doing some favors for members of your family rather than giving orders. Instead of criticizing people, tell them how much they mean to you. Don't empty your life with rules, fill it with love.

LOSE YOUR LIFE

For all the scriptural messages we hear about living the life of the Spirit, we barely appreciate what it means to actually *live* in the Spirit. And that's what today's gospel is all about. If we reflect on it long enough, we come to realize there is a little tyrant inside us that insists on living our lives for us. We call this tyrant the ego. There may be any variety of unconscious forces that affect our attitudes and behavior, but none can compare with the control that ego has over us. Meditation is a powerful technique that can lift us up to the level of Spirit, and from that elevation we can actually watch our egos in operation. Focusing us in fear about the future, taking us on guilt trips over the past, making incessant demands for petty satisfactions, the ego carries on a life of its own. And there is never satisfaction for the ego. As one writer observed, "In human life, there are only two tragedies: one is not getting what you want, and the other is getting what you want." We are set up for one disappointment or another, whatever the ego pursues.

It is to a higher Self, or Spirit, in us that Jesus is appealing when he makes the enigmatic statement recorded in the gospel of Luke: "For whoever would save his life will lose it; and whoever loses his life for my sake, he will save it." What can this mean? It was once presumed this meant we should be willing to die for Christ. Jesus, however, died for *us*, and nowhere does he intimate that his followers should die for him. What Jesus is encouraging is that we live the life of Spirit and let go the life of ego, that we lose the life of ego to save the life of Spirit. The spiritual life is a daily discipline of ego dying for the sake of living in the Spirit. In short, Jesus encourages us to let the ego rest in peace.

The ego, of course, wants no part of this. It's the ego's unswerving purpose to survive at all costs. In order to maintain its dominion, the ego tries to convince us that life can only be approached with fear, that life is a severe hardship that can only be met with relentless drive and remorseless competition, that people are basically dangerous and can only be controlled with crafty manipulations. For the ego, being frustrated, angry, anxious, even depressed, are reasonable strategies for self-preservation. Even salvation has to be "worked" at; religion is a way to "save your soul," which the ego, of course, interprets as itself.

Spirit, on the other hand, lives by a different agenda. For Spirit, life is a bounteous gift that we are to enjoy, not fear. Spirit life allows us to swim, not by thrashing in the water, but by discovering our natural buoyancy; not fighting the current, but going with the flow. Spirit knows that we are always safe in God's hands, that we "save" ourselves by "letting go," that we are most secure when we allow ourselves to be vulnerable, and that we become enriched the more we give ourselves away. We live a higher quality life, therefore, by living from the higher life of Spirit. We don't destroy the ego, but allow it to rest in peace.

Be in touch with your Spirit. Meditate in the silence of your heart and get to know your higher Self. Try to see the difference between Spirit life and ego life. Become accustomed to watching the antics of your ego. From your centered self, observe how everything the ego perceives centers on fear or guilt about one thing or another. The more determined you become to live on the level of Spirit, the more you will lose your ego and its control over your life. Live from your Spirit life. Save your life by letting your ego rest in peace.

NO EXCUSES

If there is one human activity that has become a regular feature of contemporary life, it is making excuses for one thing or another. We make excuses, and hear excuses, almost all day long. A great deal of ingenuity goes into making excuses; it has almost become an art form. With, "I got tied up in a project," a friend tries cover our disappointment that a call wasn't returned. "The car broke down" is not highly original, but is greatly in vogue as an excuse for being late for appointments. Teenagers can be particularly creative in making excuses to avoid work around the house—"coach says if I don't rest my legs all day on Saturday, it will affect my free-throws." While we like to think of ourselves as mature and accountable, we really don't like to take responsibility. Making excuses is the handiest way out.

Having a habit of making excuses makes us halfhearted, which is one of the biggest reasons why we don't feel fulfilled in life. Halfheartedness robs us of the joy and satisfaction that come from achievement. Making excuses may be an art form, but it doesn't make us feel good about ourselves. A half joke doesn't make us laugh. When workmen do a halfhearted job repairing the roof of our house, we become annoyed, and fearful of more leaks to come. When people tell us that they love us, and yet never call, or ask how we're doing, or can never agree on plans to get together, we might justifiably wonder what kind of "love" we're talking about. In the gospel reading, Jesus faces the same situation. He has obviously inspired a number of people to follow him, and his potential disciples appear to be excited about the prospect. But then the excuses start coming: "Let me first go and bury my father," or "let me first say farewell to those at my home." We can only wonder what marvelous lives these excuse-makers might have had if they didn't look back, and how much they gave up for the sake of an excuse.

Living effectively requires full-hearted commitment to our goals. No less, our religious life will be unsatisfying if we pursue it with lukewarm passion. There is much validity in the saying we might have heard often as children: "Do it right or don't do it at all." If our heart isn't in something, we're not going to do it right, or else it's going to be a "drag." In the reading from Galatians, for example, Paul says, "the whole law is fulfilled in one word, 'You shall love your neighbor as yourself.'" He is speaking about full-hearted love, love without conditions of "but," "if only," and "as long as...." Paul suggests that we will never experience the power and joy of the Christian way of life until we embrace it with all our heart and soul. This means acting out of love in all we say and do—without exception.

> Responsibility is the key word here—do what you need to do. Break the habit of making excuses for important things you need to do in your life. Never make a promise you don't intend to keep. Don't say you intend to do something when you are not committed to follow through. What needs to be done? What repairs need to be made, what jobs have you been putting off, what commitments are you falling back on? Be what you are. Be a full-time parent, or a very good friend, or an excellent worker, or a devoted Christian. What other people do is irrelevant. Become a full-hearted person and you discover a full-filling life. No excuses!

A NEW CREATION

There comes a time for every newly married couple when the honeymoon is definitely over. The end generally signals an awakening from inflated romantic fantasies. With the awakening comes the discovery that one's spouse is not perfect, cannot satisfy all one's expectations, and has features of temperament that may never have been suspected before. It is at this point that real marriage begins; it is here that a mature approach to marriage is adopted or not. Partners may skirt the issue of approaching marriage more maturely by trying to manipulate each other to fit idealized expectations, but this usually results in disappointment. The couple needs to realize that the ending of the honeymoon is a gift, a reality check, an encouragement to rise to a new way of being with a real person.

Paul faces much the same issue in his letter to the Galatians where he addresses the practice of the Christian way of life. Being human, we like to fuss over details. What is allowed and what is not? What rituals are licit and what are illicit? Which commandments are more important and which are less? What is needed to become a Christian and what prevents someone from becoming one? The only trouble with details is that we can become lost in them, and Paul recognizes this. He tells the Galatians, "For neither circumcision counts for anything, nor uncircumcision, but a new creation." What is important for a Christian is to embrace a whole new way of life.

Becoming a "new creation" essentially means we not only put off an old way of life but that we approach the Christian way of life more maturely. This means that we take our spiritual development seriously and embark on our spiritual journey from an adult perspective. This usually entails forsaking many sentimental ideas about religion we may have picked up in our training as children. We may still have childish notions about God, the purpose of our life, and what is essential to the

Christian way of living. Many of us may look upon God, for example, as a "sugar daddy" in the sky, and become angry and disillusioned with religion when God doesn't give us everything we want.

What matters is that we become "a new creation," that we embrace religion as responsible adults. We do not join a church to avoid responsibility for our salvation but to accept responsibility. Our objective in parish life should not be only to have our spiritual needs met, but to discover ways that we can meet the needs of others. We join a community of fellow believers not to gain respectability but to enter the mystery of oneness we share in the Spirit. We do not demand changes in our brothers and sisters in the faith but support them as we grow together as a loving people. Jesus loved little children, but he dealt with adults. In the gospel of Luke, he sends his disciples on a mission. It should be obvious that it was not going to be child's play.

Do a reality check on your current religious beliefs. How do you demonstrate a mature Christian life? Are you more concerned with church governance, controversies, architecture, decorations, or ritual details rather than being as loving as you can be? Are your hands routinely outstretched to get, or to give? Do you accept Jesus as the Lord of your life and are you willing to be of service to others? Never get bogged down in details at the cost of being a new creation.

WHO IS MY NEIGHBOR?

We begin this reflection with a bit of imagination. What might happen if we were on a plane, a thousand miles from nowhere, and we suddenly turned blue in the face and passed out? What if the flight attendant called for a doctor on board, but he refused to come because he was "on vacation"? What if we were being robbed in a mall parking lot, in full view of a policeman, but he refused to come to our assistance because he was "off duty"? What if a son or a daughter needed a little extra help after school but the teacher refused because "overtime is not in our contract"? How would we feel in these circumstances? In the gospel narrative of Luke, we hear the parable of the Good Samaritan. The bite in this parable is not simply people's apathy, but that the people, who by calling and profession should have helped the stricken man, were precisely the ones who passed him by. This parable is an indictment against parents who don't parent, teachers who don't teach, students who don't study, doctors who don't heal, ministers who don't minister, repairmen who don't repair, and politicians who don't work for the common good. It is also an indictment against Christians who don't perform the work of Christ in loving our neighbor as ourselves.

"And who is my neighbor?" To whom do we offer our love and care? This question is valid because most of us believe that love must be selective and carefully parceled out—after all, we have only so much to give. Furthermore, it is easy to confess love for "mankind" in general—no difficulty in that—but not so easy to love individuals, specifically. "And who is my neighbor?" The gospel provides a clear answer. Our "neighbor" is not necessarily the person next door, or people we like, or people who are fun to be with, or people listed in a parish visitation list. Love is a condition of soul; it is not selective and cannot be "parceled out." Our neighbor is *anyone* who needs us. It may be a son who is in particular need of encouragement, a student who is falling behind in lessons, a little girl lost in a store, an elderly lady across the street who cannot cut her grass, a cranky mother-in-law who has never heard a word of kindness, an uncle who has no one to talk to, the prostitute, the homosexual, the mentally disturbed, the criminal. The lesson the Lord is teaching us is that we must examine our role as Christians and be willing to perform wherever we are needed. As Christians, we are never "off duty." Whenever someone is in need of a service we can offer, we are there to provide it—no one gets passed by.

Reflect deeply on this parable of the Good Samaritan. It has a powerful lesson for Christian living. How are you "on call" as a Christian? Do you believe love has its limits? Think of the times you may have been in need and others passed you by. How did it feel? Consider the times you passed by others because of your fear, or reluctance to get involved. Love is an attitude of heart; as such, it has no limits. How loving, therefore, are you? You are not being asked to become a missionary or to search out people to serve. The people who need you are all around you every day, in your home, at work, on the streets, in your neighborhood. You will know when you are needed, so at least be willing to be of help whenever a need arises. Be who you are: a Christian in fact, as well as in name.

A MATTER OF PRIORITIES

"Life is what you make it" because life is fundamentally the result of choices we make. True, there are many circumstances in life over which we have no control, but how we allow circumstances to affect us is also a matter of our own choosing; we make or break ourselves by the attitudes and perceptions we choose to maintain. Most of our choices are good ones, because basically we are good people. Not that we don't have our failings now and then; in principle, however, we will choose good over evil. Where the real difficulty lies, however, is in making a choice among many *good* things available to us. We receive an unexpected bonus, for example, and wonder if we should spend it on new clothes, home repairs, new landscaping, a vacation, or charity. Should we buy an expensive wardrobe that will last or a less expensive one that will permit us to buy some other things? We may not make wrong choices, it's just that we might have chosen something better. How to choose what is "better" often puts us in a dilemma.

Which is what we observe in the gospel reading from Luke. Martha would fit in easily with the agenda of the modern world. She is practical, efficient, and businesslike. Her claims on Mary for help are perfectly legitimate. There is always work to be done running a household or dinner party. Have we never experienced doing all the cooking, setting up tables, serving food and drinks, and cleaning up afterwards, while someone who is supposed to be helping us is having fun with the guests? Naturally, we are resentful. When Martha complains, however, that Mary isn't doing her share of preparations, we note that Jesus does not condemn Martha for her concerns, he merely affirms that, "Mary has chosen the good portion." There is more to life than what is practical, efficient, and businesslike.

Making choices among many good options is always easier if we are clear about our priorities. What really counts in life?

What really matters? In the long run, what better serves our development and happiness? On our deathbed, what will we repent not having done? It's good to maintain a showcase home, for example, but it may be better to have a well-used one where children can play at will and friends feel completely at ease. It's good to save for a rainy day, but may be better to spend money on the present sunny one. It may be good to quit school early and go to work, but it may be better to pursue an education in order to find a good career. It is good to be highly protective of children, but it may be better for their sense of autonomy to encourage them to take some risks. It's good to find comfort in religion, but it may be better to have our faith shaken now and then so it might be revitalized. If we hope to live more effectively, choices have to be made. Priorities help us determine what the "good portion" is.

> What is it to work hard and make a lot of money, if you can't enjoy yourself? What does it mean to be successful, if you aren't happy? What good is it to build a palatial home, if no one shares it with you, or no one comes to visit? What are your priorities? What good is a gourmet meal to a hungry soul, or an impressive portfolio of investments to an empty spirit? Set up your priorities in favor of enhanced living and your spiritual development. Follow Mary's example and make choices that expand your life and help you grow.

SEEK AND FIND

We are all made equal in that no one is blessed with a problem-free life. Where we differ is in the kinds of problems we have, and especially in how we face our problems. Psychotics deny they have problems; neurotics deny that their problems are really problems. Many of us shift our problems onto others, either blaming them for our predicaments, or making them bear the effects of our poor choices. In short, we ourselves become a problem for someone else to manage. Many others go through life in the role of victim. They live resigned to their problems out of a belief that such is their lot in life. Some take consolation that this life is meant to be a "vale of tears" and look forward to happiness only in heaven.

The gospel reading provides directives for a more aggressive approach to life's challenges. In the first place, Jesus instructs us to make use of prayer to present our needs to God—the Lord's Prayer has traditionally been accepted as the perfect prayer. But resorting to prayer appears as only a prelude to what we might call Jesus's plan for affirmative action. Jesus encourages persistence, never giving up until our needs are met. His injunctions make it clear that the burden of problem-solving is our responsibility, and that it is up to us to do whatever we need to take care of ourselves. "And I tell you, ask, and it will be given you; seek, and you will find; knock and it will be opened to you." Life does not improve for the resigned and apathetic. We have our part to play. Even if our prayers are not answered according to our expectations, and even if our problems continue, we will not go unrewarded for our efforts to resolve them. "For every one who asks receives, and he who seeks finds, and to him who knocks it will be opened." Nothing we do to take care of our needs is useless. In some way, Jesus tells us, our prayers are always answered—if they are associated with *action* on our part.

Students sometimes excuse poor grades by declaring themselves "dumb." Often when asked if they actually study, they respond, "No, it wouldn't do any good." A spouse is anxious over a failing marriage and yet refuses to seek professional help. People complain of loneliness, but give no evidence that they are actively seeking to make friends. Others complain that they are bored and feel empty, yet do nothing to make changes in their life-styles or attempt to engage in something new. We can only wonder about the mediocrity and lost opportunities so many people live with because they will not ask, or seek, or knock. Effective living is chasing down opportunities, stretching oneself, setting new goals, expanding relationships; asking, seeking, knocking. The teachings of Jesus make it clear that life should not be addressed with resignation to its difficulties, but with determination and inventiveness to meet its challenges. The best things in life do not come on a platter but need to be pursued.

Never resign yourself to fate, or choose to be a victim. Pray, and then do what you need to take care of yourself. Surrendering to God's will does not mean abdicating your responsibilities to yourself. God helps those who help themselves. If you have a question, search out someone who can give you an answer; if you are confused, go to a counselor. If you feel ill, seek medical attention. If something is bothering you, get it out in the open. If your job is a dead-end street, start knocking on doors. If you need more love and affection, ask for it from those you care about. Seek, and find.

VANITY OF VANITIES

If we were to evaluate the principles governing our culture, we would likely concur that they are overtly materialistic. We are a people with a passion for things. The primary agenda for most of us is to be a consumer. Shopping malls have become new churches where we bring our needs and desires in hopes of finding salvation. Credit cards have become a new form of grace for millions. Modern advertising is the most potent preaching force in the history of mankind, and we are mesmerized by its persuasions. In terms of being influenced otherwise, we are in many respects, "limited." Mere ownership of many things, however, is not of itself a crying spiritual problem. The real problem is not that we are consumers, but that we have learned to *identify* with our possessions; our self-esteem is associated with what we own. We buy more and more in hopes of elevating our status in our own eyes and in the eyes of others. We compare what we have with what others have, and become either smug with pride, or green with envy.

All the readings today are singularly focused: they deplore any personal identification with possessions. "Vanity of vanities," cries the reading from Ecclesiastes, "All is vanity." Paul entreats the Colossians: "Set your mind on things that are above, not on things that are on earth." He bluntly calls passion for things, "idolatry." Jesus, in the gospel of Luke, stresses, "for a man's life does not consist in the abundance of his possessions." The challenge is that we come to terms with our true essence as human beings. What is our meaning and purpose? Are we primarily spiritual beings or material beings? Is it reasonable to give primary concern to satisfactions of the body which is mortal, rather than the spirit which is immortal?

Effective living means living authentically. An enriched life is living up, as best we can, to our God-given potential. But we first have to know and acknowledge who and what we are! For

Paul, of course, the answer is obvious: "Christ is all, and in all." We share the life of God's own Spirit and should therefore, "seek the things that are above." Jesus furthermore encourages us to be, "rich toward God." We need to remind ourselves often that we are more than mere matter. Our dissatisfaction, which we try so vainly to assuage with material possessions, is but our own Spirit striving to transcend our compulsion to things.

Again, this is not to disparage possessions and material comforts, but to encourage our *disengagement* from them. We are more than what we have. The truth of what we must give up at death puts the lie to any associating with what we own. Living for possessions is the root of evil and suffering. Crime is not so much the result of passion, but of unvarnished cupidity of someone else's goods. So many of our problems, our unnecessary heartaches, our long nights of worry and anxiety, are usually over *things*. We have to ask ourselves, is it worth all the suffering we endure to identify with something of such fleeting value?

Do you associate your value with your possessions; do you attempt to gain respect because of what you own? Is your credit stretched to its limit, and is your home becoming a warehouse? Be alert to what you worry about most. There is no freedom like freedom from identifying with what you own, or don't own. Be generous with what you have; practice giving things away. Put more emphasis on your spiritual life and the peace of mind that comes from simplicity. Let "Vanity of vanities" keep you in perspective.

FEAR NOT

Fear is not only one of our deepest instincts, it is generally one of our most constant companions in life. We fear all kinds of things. There are people obsessed with fear of heights, crowds, confined places, leaving the house, having dirty hands, and the like. Other fears are more commonplace. We may fear bad health, making ends meet, losing employment, what other people think, how our children will turn out. In some cases, fear is providential because it saves us from danger or getting into trouble. We do well, for example, to fear the consequences of engaging in criminal activity or insulting an employer. For the most part, however, fear is not providential but the result of certain ways of thinking that we play out in our imagination. In such cases, fear is nonproductive and crippling. Nowhere is this more obvious, for instance, than in our fear of change. Fear has little tolerance for risk and the unknown and, as such, is the single most significant factor preventing our spiritual growth and improvement in the quality of our lives.

In the gospel reading from Luke, Jesus tells us: "Fear not, little flock, for it is your Father's good pleasure to give you the kingdom." This is wonderful encouragement, but *how* do we "fear not"? How do we end fear, or at least bring it under control? To find a solution, we turn to the reading from Hebrews, where we are told: "Faith is the assurance of things hoped for, the conviction of things not seen." In other words, faith is an antidote to fear. If we truly feel *assured* in one way or another, fear disappears and the unknown ceases to be threatening. Fear can only exist where our thoughts keep us unsure of ourselves, or of the world around us. Consider for a moment how fear arises in these respects. We think poorly of ourselves, put ourselves down, refuse to acknowledge our abilities, judge ourselves primarily by what others think, and deny ourselves forgiveness for our mistakes. Self-esteem takes a constant beating; feeling we are bad and poorly equipped for life, we set ourselves up for fear. Or we think about the world: what an awful place it is, how much bad news there always is, how jumpy the economy remains, how dishonest and mean other people can be—and we are predictably fearful.

Faith, however, switches our perspective. Faith is a way of seeing. Faith allows us to look at things from a divine viewpoint and focuses our thinking according to the teachings of Jesus who assures us that, as members of the "kingdom," we have nothing to fear. Faith doesn't see things blindly, or unreasonably, it is true vision from an elevated point of view. With faith, we see ourselves as miraculous beings, intelligent, resourceful, and more than equipped by a loving God to meet our destiny in life, or any challenge life might throw our way. The world certainly has its problems, but it is still a beautiful place, with wonderful opportunities, and populated with significant numbers of caring and loving people. Is this perspective any less reasonable, or less authentic, than the negative outlook of fearful people? Is it inconceivable that we adopt this point of view and thus attain the assurance that dissolves fear?

Adopt faith as an antidote for fear. Which means, work on changing your perspective. Be aware of your thoughts and thinking patterns. See how your negative viewpoint, rather than "reality," affects your sense of security. Use the eyes of Christ when you look upon yourself, other people, and the world around you; his teachings provide a way of seeing. "It is your Father's good pleasure to give you the kingdom." From a kingdom perspective, you have nothing to fear.

CHANNEL OF GRACE

The Church celebrates the Assumption of the Virgin Mary out of belief that God specially favored her by taking her, body and soul, into heaven. She was honored in this manner because it was through her that the Word became flesh; God became incarnate through the motherhood of Mary. It was through her that the greatest grace known to mankind was ushered into the world: Jesus Christ, the Lord. But Mary is not only honored for being a vessel of God's incarnation, she is also given homage as mediatrix of countless graces that have blessed the church and millions of believers throughout the centuries. Devotions to the Mother of God manifest a faith in Mary as a channel of divine grace. We honor Mary, therefore, on this feast day, but, at the same time, we are reminded of something about ourselves: each of us, as Christians, is called upon to be a channel of grace.

The actions of human beings are never neutral. In some way, whatever we do, we affect one another. Every day of our lives, we interact with others at home, at work, in meeting with friends and acquaintances, and in a variety of casual encounters. Wherever words, feelings or actions are exchanged, some effect takes place. This effect can be positive or negative. A clerk in a supermarket, for example, can greet us with a smile, and we feel positively uplifted in mood. On the other hand, we may be busy and fail to return a phone call to a friend, with the consequence that our friend feels slighted. Life is dynamic because our actions, or inactions, have consequences. It should be a commitment on our part that we never intend to bring suffering or sorrow to another human being. We may fail at times in this resolve, but at least our heart should be in the right place.

But there is more. God works through people. We have been chosen to be vessels through which the grace of God flows. As Christians, we are called to build God's kingdom; our mission is not only not to harm others, but to pour love into their lives.

Each of us has the ability to bring grace into the lives of others. Our love is divine energy, and we should never discount its power. Unconditional love for our children enhances their self-esteem. Showing a little gratitude to people makes them feel appreciated and encourages them to share more of their own love. Supportive comments we make at work can help fellow workers feel energized; words of encouragement can bring comfort to those facing difficult times. If we can make people laugh, we raise their levels of joy. If we can offer wise advice, we help people in despair see options for resolving their problems. It isn't uncommon that an offer to lend a helping hand turns cold cynicism into warm trust about the basic goodness of life and other people. We honor Mary today, therefore, but also our own capacity to be a channel of grace.

> Examine your behavior. Does what you do allow God to work through you? God has chosen you as a vessel of divine love. See yourself as a channel of grace. Recognize the power you have to bring hope, healing, encouragement, and joy to others. Work miracles with your love. Never let a day pass that you don't do something to improve the quality of life of people around you. Opportunities are unlimited, especially when are willing to lend a hand. Open your channel.

TWENTIETH SUNDAY IN ORDINARY TIME
Jeremiah 38:4–6, 8–10 Hebrews 12:1–4 **Luke 12:49–53**

COMFORTABLE RELIGION

Priests and ministers consider giving comfort to those in distress one of the most important functions of their office. People are in need of comfort when facing illness, loss of a loved one, or some other misfortune. Many Christians affirm that religion is one of their greatest comforts in life. Moreover, many become disturbed and offended when the comforting aspects of religion are unsettled. Some church members become upset, for example, when church leaders become involved in political and social issues, or when a pastor promotes involvement in environmental concerns, or the rights of minorities. While "fire and brimstone" preachers retain popularity, they are generally not appreciated by the great bulk of believers, who prefer preachers to "say nice things," and "make people happy." After all, Jesus was known for the comfort he brought people. Didn't he proclaim: "Peace I leave you; my peace I give you"?

The gospel, however, makes it clear that Jesus proclaimed other things as well. The narrative records words of Jesus that can only be called alarming to our religious comfort zones. "I came to cast fire upon the earth; and would that it were already kindled! ... Do you think that I have come to give peace on earth? No, I tell you, but rather division." It pays us to remember that Jesus was considered an agitator by political and religious leaders of his time. At times, even his disciples found him too much to bear and walked away from him. In the minds of his executioners, Jesus was not crucified for his comforting words. Furthermore, we need to remind ourselves that Christianity was founded on a cross, not at a board meeting. The early Christians suffered terribly for their beliefs, and many went to their deaths because of their convictions. The Church has known many persecutions throughout its history, and persecutions were often drafted by governments because of threats they saw in Christian beliefs. We might ask ourselves what "menace" was perceived.

We love our comforts. More money is spent every year for personal comforts than has been donated to the church in its history. We like our religion to be comfortable and our grace to be cheap. The gospel is not meant to endorse "fire and brimstone," or to deny the authentic place that giving comfort has in Christian ministry, but it does remind us that the Christian mission has a broader agenda. If anything, the gospel intends to shake up our complacency. The effects of religion on society today are questionable. Why has Christianity lost its bite? We need to be wary of religion that only makes us feel good. We should not be upset when church leaders take up the cause of the poor, the forgotten, and the outcast. It should inspire us to see the Christian parents rally to the cause of religious education of children and not leave character formation to *Sesame Street*, or the streets of the neighborhood. There are times we need comfort, but there are also times we need "fire."

What expectations do you have of religion? How do you feel when you find church people taking a stand on social issues? Do you believe religion should remain "private"? On a more personal level, have you grown spiritually over the years? Do you find yourself challenged by the gospels and the preaching that interprets them? If you find the practice of religion easy, you might consider whether you truly understand your faith. If the gospel doesn't shake you up now and then, you might consider whether you are truly listening.

DISCIPLINE

Politicians always get roaring applause when they speak about the freedoms we are entitled to. "Freedom" is one of our most cherished channels for happiness. We not only demand freedom from oppression, but also from an expectation of doing things one way. We want freedom to be what we want to be, go where we want to go, say what we want to say, and do what we want to do. Anything that threatens our freedom puts us immediately on the defensive; from childhood on, we have little stomach for restrictions of any kind. This poses a problem. As affluence increases, and as technology and human inventiveness provide us more and more conveniences, we tend to become spoiled. For many of us, there is one more freedom in big demand: freedom from effort.

"Effort," and its companion "discipline," are falling out of use in our culture's vocabulary. Our preoccupation with freedom leads us to believe that everything we have a taste for should be ours by right, and that everything we want should come to us easily. We don't like to hear about hardship and are impatient with talk about patience. Children, for example, subjected to relentless doses of contemporary advertising, have a difficult time postponing gratification for anything. It's hard to get students to concentrate on studies. Laborers consistently go on strike for more money for less work. Young couples don't want to have to struggle starting out in marriage; they want immediately what it took their parents years to achieve. We want what we want, and we want it now! But while we want a better life for ourselves, we are increasingly reluctant to pay for it.

The reading from Hebrews exhorts us not to make light of discipline. And with good reason. It is perfectly legitimate to aspire to freedom, but we can enjoy freedom only if we accept limits. What good is freely indulging our desires, for example, if it reaches a point where they enslave us in addiction and destroy our health? Furthermore, we can only make use of the freedom to pursue a better life for ourselves if we are willing to discipline ourselves to make the efforts to achieve it. The irony is that everybody wants something for nothing in a society where everything good costs. Life can be "a bowl of cherries," but, for the most part, only for those willing to pick them. To be physically fit, for instance, we have to work at it. To live comfortably in a good house will require generous hours of maintenance. To have a satisfying marriage or friendship will demand commitment, tact, flexibility, and endurance. Freedom, therefore, is important, but it goes hand-in-hand with discipline. Self-respect is knowing we can control our impulses, delay our gratifications, and make the efforts required to attain what we want out of life. Spiritual growth always requires discipline, especially when we are called upon to give up whatever holds back our development and to persevere in the struggle to attain our goals.

The reading from Hebrews suggests that discipline is good for us. If the idea of discipline makes you feel uncomfortable, you may need a change in attitude if you hope to improve the quality of your life. Accept discipline as a perfectly legitimate part of living; see it in a positive light. Effort can be just as enjoyable as the goal it pursues. Make the effort that is required to expand your horizons, actualize your talents, grow in self-respect, develop supportive relationships, have a good marriage, keep good friends, and the like. Freedom certainly provides *opportunity*, but only discipline offers hope for *achievement*.

HUMILITY

Arrogant people are irritating. Few things annoy us more than people who think they are better than we are, acquaintances who put on airs, or someone trying to show off. Among all the shortcomings we observe in others, there is something in us that sees pride as particularly offensive. Perhaps that's the reason why we love hearing about scandals. Nothing piques our attention like gossip; the juicier the details of someone else's humiliation, the more avidly we listen. Much as we might like to deny it, don't we enjoy the spectacle of a popular figure, a movie star, or a politician falling from grace? In the gospel reading, we hear Jesus speaking about someone at a marriage feast seating himself in a place of prominence, only to be asked to move lower when someone more eminent arrives. Aren't we secretly amused at seeing someone's bubble burst?

Our strong sentiments against pride might lead us to conclude that we honor humility, even that we ourselves are humble. When Jesus, for example, concludes his parable with, "For every one who exalts himself will be humbled, and he who humbles himself will be exalted," we might agree with him completely. After all, life provides plenty of examples of how the proud are humbled and how the humble are exalted. We need to be cautious, however, about the state of our humility because life also provides many examples of how subtly pride can introject itself. The very fact, for instance, that we are irritated by overtly proud people shows that we have our pride. Doesn't annoyance with opinionated coworkers come from pride in our own opinions? Do we not demonstrate pride when we get into arguments and have to prove that we are right? Whenever we react to criticism, isn't it pride that makes us defensive? Pride can even display itself in a reluctance to change. We can observe this in an insistence that "I don't have any problem," or "I don't need anybody's help," or "I'm just fine the way I am." We don't have to be a "show off" to demonstrate pride, sometimes all we have to be is stubborn.

This does not, however, discount appropriate pride we should take in our achievements. To live effectively requires that we esteem and enjoy the fruits of our efforts to make a better life for ourselves. Healthy pride is one that is spiritually well-placed; it is not arrogant, and can energize us to continue our spiritual growth. We need to remember that misguided humility can keep us down on ourselves and our abilities, mired in self-defeating beliefs, entrenched in bad habits, and blind to opportunities for personal development. In short, "humility" is often a disguise for lack of self-esteem; it can be just as disastrous to our well-being as arrogance.

When you ritually examine your conscience for sins, do you ever find any? If your spouse, or your children, calls something you do into question, are you "impossible to talk to"? If you don't know what you are talking about, are you inclined to keep quiet? For all the times you may have offended another, how often do you apologize? Humble yourself by loving the truth at all costs, and by always being willing to learn. Show humility in your willingness to change. Take appropriate pride in your hard work and accomplishments. Relish the fact that you are a child of God and a member of the body of Christ. Demonstrate that pride in the love you share with everyone you encounter.

DETACHMENT

The words of Jesus in the gospel reading are very disturbing. We might wonder if Luke isn't seriously misquoting the Lord. One after another, admonitions are thrown at us that seem an affront to common sense, if not the central message of the gospels. Are we to take Jesus at his word when he says, "If any one comes to me and does not hate his own father and mother and wife and children and brothers and sisters, yes, and even his own life, he cannot be my disciple"? Can Jesus be serious when he proclaims, "So therefore, whoever of you does not renounce all that he has cannot be my disciple"? Are we to actually "hate" those who mean so much to us, and give up "all" we own, in order to be authentically Christian?

How is it that popular fundamentalist preachers escape these stinging prescriptions for discipleship? Many are renowned for their love of family and for their extensive possessions. In light of this reading, would Jesus condone Rolls Royces, million dollar condos, private jets, and clothes that might adorn royalty? How do we explain the possessions of the church? Would golden chalices, elaborate buildings, priceless works of art, ostentatious liturgies, and the like win approval from Christ? Jesus had no possessions of any mention; he admitted he had no place of his own to lay his head. He had a special fondness for the poor and proclaimed that it was easier for a camel to pass through the eye of a needle than for a rich man to enter the kingdom. And yet Jesus had friends who sustained him in his ministry; there was a "purse" that Jesus shared with his disciples; there is never any mention that Jesus condemned his wealthier supporters. He also spoke of love as the cornerstone of the kingdom. Can we imagine Jesus "hating" his own mother? How are we to interpret his statements?

It is important to keep in mind that what Jesus primarily called for in his followers was not "hatred" of anyone, but a conversion of attitude, a change of heart. What mattered most was becoming a loving person. Anything that would hinder the freedom, openness, and outgoingness of love would need to be abandoned for a new way of life. What Jesus is asking us to renounce are our *dependencies and attachments.* It's one thing, for example, to love members of our family—and anyone else for that matter—and quite another to be so dependent on them that we never develop our uniqueness, or hear the call to our own destiny. It is one thing to have possessions, and quite another to be so attached to them that they become our whole life. Being well-to-do is not of itself a sin, and poverty is not automatically a virtue. There are wealthy people who are generous to a fault; there are also poor people who wouldn't part with a glass of water. In the mind of Jesus, it's all a matter of where our heart is.

Where is your heart? Do your relationships with others help, or prevent, you from being a true disciple of Christ? How do you view the things you own? Are you so concerned about your possessions that little else matters in life, especially the state of your soul? What might you need to renounce to fulfill your Christian destiny and become a more loving person? Is it your vindictiveness, laziness, stubbornness; your need to have the last word or have things always go your way? Might you even need to renounce your depression, always feeling sorry for yourself, or thinking only of your own problems? Be willing to detach yourself from *whatever* restricts your loving spirit.

WHEN THEY'RE READY

One of our favorite things to do with other people is try to change them. We sincerely believe we know what is good for others. It is especially difficult watching someone we love throw his or her life away in an unpromising marriage proposal, in an addiction, or in missing golden opportunities, because they won't see the obvious and take our advice. We're good people; we've learned wisdom from hard experience; our intentions are noble in wanting to help others avoid unnecessary pitfalls in their lives—if only they would listen! Our hearts go out to the father of the prodigal son in the gospel reading. The young son wants to break away from home and abruptly asks his father to give him his whole inheritance. The son then goes off to squander his inheritance in wild living, and soon finds himself utterly destitute. Couldn't all this pain have been avoided?

The parable of the prodigal son is a compelling story of forgiveness and is often interpreted as an example of how God lovingly forgives us when we fall from grace—"I tell you, there will be more joy in heaven over one sinner who repents than over ninety-nine righteous persons who need no repentance." True enough, but there is another great lesson in this parable. We note that the father of the prodigal son didn't refuse his son's request for the inheritance—as he might have. He did not browbeat him into remaining at home or threaten him with dire predictions over his potential folly. The father simply let him go; he did not try to change his son's intentions, foolish as they might be. As a result, the son went off and learned his lessons from his own experience. He enjoyed the good life for a while, suffered from his squandering, and discovered how good he had it back at home. Which was not the case of the other brother who obviously didn't appreciate how good he had it. Full of resentment over his younger brother's return, he had nothing but complaints to his father for not receiving special attention.

We want what's best for those we love, but are we willing to admit that it is impossible to change people until they are *ready?* As a matter of fact, we cannot change other people at all; when they are ready for change, they have already changed. As experience bears out, we sometimes have to go through a personal hell to learn important lessons. Often all we can do is support others with our love, and hope they learn their lessons without suffering too much damage. Isn't this the lesson of the prodigal son? Isn't this the way God is with us? God lets us make our mistakes, and learn our lessons, even if it's the hard way. God ever supports us with love, is willing to wait patiently until we are ready to correct our ways, and is then prepared to welcome us back with joy. No matter the "obvious," no matter how much we love, we cannot teach others to learn what they need to learn on their own, in their own time.

Have you ever succeeded in "making" someone change? Do you believe you can change someone's heart by commanding their behavior? How willing are you to let others learn their own lessons, even when you think they are headed for trouble? Can you pretend to know what is best for anyone? No matter how good your intentions, can you really define what is someone else's "own good?" Allow people to own their own lives, and their own mistakes. You cannot live other people's lives for them. Live your own life, and be content that what's "best" for others is the support of your unconditional love.

LITTLE THINGS COUNT

If there's one thing the media has a talent for, it is creating the spectacular. New shows on television are introduced with enormous fanfare to lead us to conclude that we have never seen anything like it before. It takes great craft to hold our attention. News has become so monotonously repetitious that unpretentious stories have to be editorially exaggerated to appear as high drama. Our culture is forever trying to convince us that "more" is better and that "bigger" is best. Consequently, we draw conclusions that we will find substance in quantity, and quality in excess. We tend to assume, for example, that someone must be important if they are driving a very expensive car. It takes heroic proportions to impress us. As a result, we take little things for granted, and may even put ourselves down as second-rate because we can't impress others.

The gospel reading reminds us that little things count too. The heroic may impress us, but we should also be impressed by the ordinary. We are moved by a fireman risking his life to save an infant from a burning building, but we can also be moved by hardworking parents who make little sacrifices every day to provide a good education for their children. It's remarkable to see a basketball star sign a multimillion-dollar contract, but what about a custodian who keeps the halls of an apartment building spotless and the landscaping beautified with flowers? Little things are the building blocks of greater things, and they can't be discounted. Our bodies, for instance, may be large, but they are composed of millions of tiny cells, any and all of which can must function properly to keep us in good health. Jesus says: "He who is faithful in very little is faithful also in much; and he who is dishonest in a very little is dishonest also in much." How we handle the little things in our lives indicates how we will handle larger issues. For example, we will never fulfill our Christian calling to become loving people if we can't show ordinary courtesy to fellow workers.

We may be disappointed that our life is not more exciting, or that our income is not in a higher tax bracket, or that we don't have the clout to make needed changes in society, but we need to reflect that making comparisons is only a game. Everything we do out of love is important. An encouraging word to a teenager can change the direction of his life. Holding back criticism can make a coworker feel good about herself. A simple act of charity can convince a homeless man not to end his life. Sending a greeting card to an old friend might bring her out of depression. Little things count. Daily life has its repetitious routines and the major part of our working day is dealing with the commonplace. But each day of our lives can be ennobled by the loving attention we put into everything we do: keeping our homes happy, doing the best we can in our jobs, asking about a neighbor's sick infant, making small talk with an elderly widow, volunteering to do the dishes. Anything done out of love is impressive.

> Consider the multiple opportunities you have every day to bring some love into the lives of others. There is nothing you do that can't be done in a loving manner. Doing laundry, for example, and preparing meals can be labors of love. Resolve to perform your daily duties with more care-filled attention. Go out of your way to be pleasant. Love is often demonstrated by heroic sacrifice, but more often by consistent, loving attention to small details.

TWENTY-SIXTH SUNDAY IN ORDINARY TIME
Amos 6:1a, 4–7 1 Timothy 6:11–16 **Luke 16:19–31**

WILLPOWER

Personal success and getting ahead in life are usually associated with willpower and determination. People who are aggressive, dominating, ruggedly individualistic, high achievers are credited with possessing a strong will. By the same token, those who are passive, dependent, easily manipulated, and low achieving are spoken of as weak-willed. The implication is that we are temperamentally endowed with a certain amount of willpower and that there isn't much we can do about it. Many of us may believe, consequently, that our potential in life is limited and that there are limits on what we can do to change ourselves for the better. Think, for example, of acquaintances who say: "I can't stop smoking," "I just can't stick to a diet," "I'm too old to change," or "I just don't have the willpower." Lack of willpower is one of the most commonly given excuses for a host of bad habits, lack of achievement, and even sinful ways.

The gospel reading from Luke, however, suggests that lack of willpower is not an excuse for living ineffectively or irresponsibly. In the parable of Jesus, we come to know the fate of a rich man who dies and is punished in Hades for having lived a selfish and profligate life. In his torments, the rich man has compassion for his brothers who are living just as wantonly, and he asks Abraham to send Lazarus back from the dead to warn them to repent. Abraham makes the observation: "If they do not hear Moses and the prophets, neither will they be convinced if some one should rise from the dead." What Abraham is saying in our context is not that the rich man's brothers are too weak-willed to change, but that they are *obstinate*. They wouldn't change for anybody, no matter who it was warning them. What this demonstrates is that stubbornness is one of the clearest manifestations of willpower in the world—and we are all fully endowed with it.

Have we ever tried taking candy from a baby, or a toy from a small child? It is easy to witness raw willpower even in an infant. Teenagers who can't build up enough determination to do schoolwork or household chores may also display tenacious resistance to advice given by their parents. An employer who insists he has no willpower to quit smoking may also display an "iron fist" in running his company. Stubborn determination is an excellent example of willpower. It should teach us that, if we have plenty of willpower to be resistant, or to do what we *like* to do, it follows to reason that we have the same willpower within to do whatever else we want. And that is the key word—we do what we really "want" to do. Willpower is energized automatically in proportion to our true wants and desires, be it resistance or positive action. If we have the willpower to be obstinate, we have the willpower to do anything we set our mind to.

You may not want to change, and that is certainly your option, but don't pretend you are victimized by insufficient willpower. You will always find enough strength to do what you really *want* to do. Reflect on situations in your life where you demonstrate great strength of will, especially in terms of being stubborn. You have more willpower than you imagine. Focus on your objectives and do what needs to be done. Transfer the power of your stubbornness into determination to change something about yourself for the better, or make a better life for yourself. Use your power to overcome obstacles, and make your dreams come true.

EMPOWER YOURSELF

We enjoy settling into our routines and like it when things come easy for us. We're generally on the lookout for shortcuts, for ways to get around work, and for whatever makes life more comfortable. We look for the easy way out of difficult situations; if a little lie, for example, can help us avoid a confrontation, we'll use it. The more obligations we can toss off our shoulders, the better we feel. Who needs hassles? At the same time, however, we also feel the impulse to make a better life for ourselves. Something within us pushes us to dream our dreams, be ambitious, make resolutions, and become antsy with sitting still. There is obviously a tug-of-war going on within us that at one moment wants to keep us settled and the next moment to find some excitement. What is it within us that shakes our apathy and unsettles our lethargy?

Paul, in his letter to Timothy, gives us an answer. We are fundamentally spirits having a human experience in a body. The body may like its routines and comforts, and an easy way out of responsibilities, but the spirit has another agenda. The spirit is not inclined to sit back as a passive spectator; it relentlessly urges us on to bigger and better things. Paul minces no words when he says: "for God did not give us a spirit of timidity but a spirit of power and love and self-control." Our spirit is pure power; as an energy source, it is always operational and inexhaustible. We need never fear that we are powerless to do what we need to do to take care of ourselves, or achieve whatever goals we set for ourselves; spirit is limitless in what it can accomplish. What Paul encourages us to do, therefore, is *access* the spirit. Like plugging into an electrical outlet, when we access spirit, we empower ourselves. This is what it means to become enthused and excited. And this is precisely what Jesus means, in the gospel of Luke, when he says: "If you had faith as a grain of mustard seed, you could say to this sycamore tree, 'Be rooted up, and be planted in the sea,' and it would obey you." What is "faith" but another word for spirit operating on its limitless possibilities? The tiniest amount of faith, or spirit, can work miracles.

There *is* a tug-of-war going on within us between laziness and enthusiasm, and we always have a choice about what side of that tug-of-war we wish to join. If we focus on how tired we are, on how bad we feel, on how many problems we have, on how badly things are going, is it any wonder that we want to crawl into a hole and hide? On the other hand, if we focus on challenge rather than fear, on the power of our love, on our innate ability for self-control, on our God-given capacity to solve our problems, and our past experiences of achievement, can we not expect to find a renewal of energy and confidence? We are not without means for handling any hardship, or accomplishing for ourselves whatever we want. A slight shift in focus may be all we need to get us moving.

Consider the times you may have found your second wind after an exhausting day at work, perhaps to meet with an old friend who just got into town, or go out to a night baseball game. Where did your energy come from? Reflect on the power of your spirit and learn to get in touch with its vigor. *Focus* on what you want to do; concentrate on all the wonderful benefits that will come from doing it. Your faith focus can move mountains for you, as long as you pursue what you desire with unflagging confidence in your spiritual power.

WHERE ARE
THE OTHER NINE?

It is likely we have experienced going out of our way to help someone without receiving so much as an acknowledgment or word of thanks for our efforts. It probably left us with a bitter taste. We may develop compassion for other people's faults, but it is especially difficult to handle ingratitude. In the gospel reading, we are told that Jesus cured ten lepers of a loathsome disease, and only one returned to give him thanks. Jesus asks, "Where are the nine?" We might ask the same question, and wonder what response the nine would offer to excuse their obvious display of ungratefulness. Perhaps some were so excited about being cured that they forgot the one who cured them. Maybe others felt Jesus was just "doing his job" as a wonder worker, and didn't need any thanks. Whatever the excuse, the ingratitude is blatant.

The gospel narrative should encourage us to ask ourselves how much ingratitude plays a part in our own lives. Admittedly, none of us would ever want to *appear* ungrateful, but ingratitude can take on subtle forms. In the first place, gratefulness does not come to us automatically. As children, we had to be *taught* to say "thank you," and it is difficult to completely abandon a childhood belief that we are the center of the universe and that life owes us. Furthermore, most of us are uncomfortable with feeling "obligated." We like to settle our debts quickly, and don't want to be "beholden" to anyone. It is easy, therefore, to become hardened into thinking that we are independent of others and are indebted only to ourselves for our accomplishments. We may take pride, for example, that we are "self-made," and that everything we have achieved for ourselves is purely the result of our talents and industriousness. In this light, many see their interactions with others as merely a business of "give and take," for which no thanks are necessary. Finally, it is also easy to become so busy with daily activities that we simply have no time to reflect on the good things we have. We don't feel thankful because we simply don't pay attention to things we need to be thankful for.

Thankfulness is not a once-in-a-while response for having received a favor, it is an attitude of soul, a readiness always to give thanks. Gratitude is an attitude that springs from a heart that senses *everything* in life as a gift. This attitude necessitates a shift from self-centeredness to looking beyond self. When we can acknowledge that we are part of a great web of life, and are touched by grace from countless sources, our life can change dramatically. We see this in the reading from Kings, for example, where Naamen the Syrian is so full of gratitude for the grace of his cure, he switches his allegiance from his gods to the one God of Israel. Once we transcend self-preoccupation, we begin to see that our minds, our bodies, our talents, our very existence, are all gifts, lovingly bestowed on us. Expansion of vision permits us to be permanently grateful.

> Consider the great number of people without whom you could not sustain yourself, even the life to which you have become accustomed. What would your life be like without the love and support you receive from family and friends? Do you take too much for granted? Think of all the people who have had an impact on your development, who have taught you, inspired you, given you opportunities, forgiven you, healed you. Consider even the valuable lessons you have learned from difficult people and hardships you have faced. You have "everything in the world" to be thankful for, and should never hesitate to go back to say "thank you."

AS LONG AS IT TAKES

It is essential to the concept of capitalism that there always be something new to buy and sell. A flourishing economic market is dependent on obsolescence, new products, quick turnover, and fresh marketing schemes. Fashions change with the seasons; advertising creates new tastes; plastics make it easy to throw things away. There are also turnovers in politics, styles of living, home decorating, "healthy" diets, even religious values and practices. Not a day goes by without an assumption being reinforced that "nothing lasts." Furthermore, in an ever-quickening pace of life, we have developed little tolerance for delays. We've grown to expect quick solutions to our problems and immediate gratification of our needs; relief doesn't sell unless it is "instant." Consequently, persevering is not easy for us. Rather than wait in line, for example, we leave.

While we may be accustomed to the dynamics of quick turnover and demands for instant relief, we need to be aware of how this affects us spiritually. Believing "nothing lasts" makes us less prepared to make, or keep, commitments. The high divorce rate, for example, demonstrates that many couples would rather end marriage than work out their conflicts. Why keep pushing when our dreams remain unfulfilled? Why put effort into doing a good job, making sacrifices, or working to make a better life for ourselves, if we can't see results? Why continue to pray if our prayers don't seem to be answered?

All three readings today speak, in one way or another, about the value of perseverance. In Exodus, we see that Israel prevails in battle only as long as Moses keeps his arms outstretched. Paul encourages Timothy to remain firm in his faith as he pursues a difficult ministry. The reading from Luke relates a parable of Jesus, "to the effect that they ought always to pray and not lose heart." The parable demonstrates the rewards of persistence: an unrighteous judge rules in favor of a widow who perseveres in her appeals for vindication against an adversary. The lesson in these readings is that commitments should be kept, and that perseverance is the key to success in any endeavor. Joy may be found in the pleasures of the moment, but true happiness is only found in something of permanence. Remaining faithful to commitments is invaluable for our self-respect and happiness, especially when we stick by them through difficult times. Marriage, for example, reserves its choicest blessings for couples who have persevered through its lows as well as its highs. Furthermore, we never achieve our goals of a better life for ourselves unless we follow through on our resolutions. Success is only promised to those willing to do "whatever it takes," for "as long as it takes." We find answers to our prayers, for example, not by demanding immediate responses, but by persevering in storming the gates of heaven.

Do you have any principles or beliefs that anchor your life and give it substance? Are you a "pushover" when it comes to advertising and trends? Have you made up your own mind on what you really need to be happy in life? Do you see the value for your self-esteem in keeping your commitments? Can you appreciate how you demonstrate character in the way you keep faith throughout difficult times? Keep the faith. Never discount the importance of perseverance. Some things take time. Be willing to fight for what you think is important—for "as long as it takes."

Does Prayer Work?

Most of us learned from the time we were children that prayer was not only a way to praise God, but a means of getting our needs met. Scripture is full of admonitions that we pray; belief in the power of prayer appears to be unquestionable. In the reading from Sirach, we are told that, "He whose service is pleasing to the Lord will be accepted, and his prayer will reach to the clouds." In the gospel we hear the parable about the publican and the pharisee who went to the temple to pray. The prayer of the publican pleased God, and, Jesus informs us, the man was "justified." The question is, are we justified in believing that prayer really works? Cannot we give many examples where our prayer wasn't answered? Does God really answer our prayers?

It is also clear from Scripture that there needs to be a quality to our prayer for it to be effective. Sirach has no doubt that our prayers are answered but he also informs us that prayer needs to be humble; it is the prayer "of the humble" that pierces the clouds. In the parable of the publican and the pharisee, the pharisee doesn't pray, he brags! The prayer of the publican justified him because it was humble. We need to consider the element of humility, therefore, in any question of whether prayer "works" or not. In the first place we need to recognize a subtle arrogance that may enter our praying. In much of what we pray for, we assume we know more about what we need than God does. We approach prayer with our agendas and expectations and are disappointed when responses don't come forth according to our timetables. Experience shows that many things we once prayed for passionately were not good for us; we may be grateful now that some of our prayers weren't answered. Perhaps we've discovered that getting what we earnestly prayed for caused us misfortunes we never anticipated. Not everyone sails into a happy life after winning the lottery.

119

And there are other factors that affect the quality of our prayer. Sometimes we approach prayer as a business deal; if God will answer a prayer, we promise to change something in our lives, or do God a favor—"Take away this cancer, Lord, and I will go to church every Sunday." We may even ask for the things in complete disregard of our own responsibilities to take care of ourselves—"Take these pounds off me, Lord." Finally, sometimes we approach prayer halfheartedly; if our prayers are not immediately answered, we give up on them, forgetting that lack of perseverance generally proves we don't really want what we pray for.

God does answer humble prayer, and there is good reason we offer prayers on our knees. Humility allows us to trust that God loves us immeasurably, that God cares for us with ever watchful eyes, that God knows what is best for us, and that God is pleased to provide what lies in our best interest. Scripture often makes reference that we should pray "always." What this suggests is that humble prayer is finally an attitude, a way of relating to God on a permanent basis. We are prayer-full when we surrender ourselves to God's love, accepting all that happens to us as part of God's plan. With such an attitude, no prayer is unanswered.

Reflect on your attitudes in prayer. Do you use prayer as an escape from personal responsibility for yourself? Are you putting more hope in your prayer than in God? Are you telling God what to do, proposing a bargain, rather than surrendering to God's will? Make your prayer humble; it will put you in the right frame of mind. Above all, listen to God when you pray. Even God's silence may be an answer to your prayers.

PURE OF HEART

The feast of All Saints is a Christian form of hero worship. We celebrate this feast day by paying homage to the men, women, and children noted for their holiness and exemplary practice of the Christian way of life. Their lives encourage us to appreciate that living according to the teachings of Jesus may be difficult, but it is not beyond our reach. All of us have received the call of Christ to follow him in building the kingdom of God. God does not invite us to a task beyond our ability; God promises to give us everything we need to accomplish our destiny. This feast day is a reminder that we too are called to be saints.

But how can we be saints? Is not aspiring to sainthood pretentious? Yes, we want to lead a good life, but how many of us feel called to, much less capable of, heroics? Realistically, what can we have in common with the great saints in history? The question is a good one: what *do* saints have in common? At first glance, when we study the lives of the saints, nothing much in common is revealed. The church's catalogue of saints includes a remarkable range of characters, temperaments, and professions. Some saints were young and some very old; some died violent deaths as martyrs, some died peacefully in advanced age. Some were highly educated, some not at all. Some saints were valiant warriors, others were monks and nuns who never left the peaceful confines of their monasteries and convents. We find saints who were clergy and others who were laity; scholars and others who were farmers; rulers of nations and others who were wanderers with no place of their own. But, searching a little deeper, we find a quality that does set saints apart. What saintly men and women of all times have had in common was *purity of heart*. And, as Jesus tells us in the gospel reading, "Blessed are the pure in heart, for they shall see God." The saints were holy because they saw God, and walked in the presence of God. People were acknowledged as saints, not only because of their good deeds, but because, when people had an encounter with a saintly person, they left feeling they had been in God's presence.

But what does it mean to be "pure of heart," and where do we "see" God? The answer is revealed when we understand something about our spiritual nature. There is utter goodness at the center of our being where our spirit is to be found. Despite the endless distractions that make us believe we are exclusively part of a material world, we are spirits, sharing the one Spirit of God. To fully accept our inner spirit as part of God's own life is to have a pure heart—no matter our faults and weaknesses. To see ourselves deeply as we truly are, is to see God. To live the life of our inner spirit is to live in holiness. By our very nature, therefore, we are saints. That is why the reading from John so boldly proclaims: "Beloved, we are God's children now." We are holy when we live who we are.

Get in touch with your spirit. Go into your center often and, in quiet meditation, come to know yourself as spirit. Recognize that the essence of your life is the Spirit of God who dwells within you. This will make you pure of heart, and allow you to see God. Don't say that sainthood is impossible for you, or that aspiring to holiness is pretentious. With all your heart, accept yourself as a "child of God," not as a pious thought, but as literal truth. Commit yourself to a life and behavior that will manifest the presence of God in you. You don't have to do anything heroic to demonstrate holiness—just be yourself!

ALL THE FAITHFUL DEPARTED (ALL SOULS)
Wisdom 3:1–9 Romans 6:3–4, 8–9 John 11:21–27

DEATH'S GIFT
OF MEANING

We live in a death-denying culture. Death, and the prospect of dying, are not topics for polite conversation; many people don't even want to talk about making out a will. Hospitals, nursing homes, and especially funeral parlors may make us uncomfortable; they hit too close to home with reminders of mortality. Youthfulness is adored in our society, and billions of dollars are spent every year on products promising to make us look young again. Even in death we try to escape its finality; at wakes, great efforts are made to make the deceased look as alive and vibrant as possible. It is foolish, however, to deny, or ignore, the inevitable; we begin our journey toward death from the moment we are born. The feast of All the Faithful Departed not only prayerfully reminds us of loved ones who have died before us, but of our own mortality. As we honor those who have gone before us, we are also encouraged to honor our own death.

The problem with avoiding thinking about our death is that it deprives us of an important perspective. Many of the mistakes we make in life are the result of a pretense that we will go on forever in this world. Maybe, for example, we jeopardize our health with poor diets and risky addictions. Perhaps we exhaust ourselves by living beyond our means, or by killing ourselves with work for things we don't need, or by being so busy with commitments that we never have time for ourselves. Much of the emotional distress we suffer is the result of exaggerating our expectations and disappointments. When we attach inflated value to the passing events in our lives, or to what other people do, we develop anxieties that erode away our happiness. Reflecting on death, however, causes us to reevaluate our purposes. From the perspective of death, meanings change dramatically. Acknowledging the prospect of our death, we begin to see things quite differently.

Dying people generally experience a reshuffling of values and priorities. Preoccupations, worries of one kind or another, petty arguments, age-old resentments, a bout with the flu, and the like don't seem as important anymore. On the other hand, the dawning of a new day, the smiles of loved ones, the laughter of friends, a walk in the park, a bouquet of flowers take on significant importance. With death, things are put into perspective. When we better appreciate the inevitability of death, we appreciate life more. When we accept our death, we can accept other people, and difficult situations, with more compassion and forbearance. In the final analysis, the prospect of death is a great leveler of exaggerations, and of things that simply don't matter in the long run. It permits us to live with more tranquility and peace of mind.

> Remember the faithful departed with prayer and recollection of fond memories; reflect on their lives and what they meant to you. Be thankful for the love they shared with you and for the lessons you learned from your relationship with them. Spend some moments reflecting on your own death. Picture yourself on your dying day and try to imagine what you might lament not having done in your lifetime. What do you suspect you'll repent of? Today is the beginning of the rest of your wonderful life. Reassess your priorities. What is important, and what is not? Make some changes in your life-style that reflect a sensible acceptance of the inevitability of your death. Change your fear of dying into love of living. Let everything you do reflect how seriously you take that love.

WELCOME THE OUTCAST

It's ironic that, while the world is becoming a smaller place, people today feel more lonely and alienated from one another than ever before. Neighborhood communities aren't what they used to be; even families don't retain the close ties they enjoyed only a few generations ago. People who can afford to, build up all kinds of barriers to insure their privacy. Many of us have no desire to be involved with community, and prefer to be left alone. Not that we become hermits, only that, if we gather for socializing, we prefer to be with "our own kind." By the same token, we are also inclined to view people who are not "one of us" as aliens and outcasts. In a highly pluralistic society such as ours, we might expect more forbearance, if not delight, for people who are different from us. But such is not the case. Racial tensions continue their ebb and flow and modern communications seem to expose us to more groups and individuals to dislike. Security is a primary concern for millions today. Rather than appreciate differences, we tend to view more and more people as threats.

The gospel reading addresses separation, and our tendency to see others who are different from us as outcasts. Jesus provides an example that challenges us to a basic change in attitude. One of the biggest complaints of the opponents of Jesus was over the kind of people he chose to associate with. For a religious figure, Jesus regularly hung around the wrong crowd. He dined with people who were known to be public sinners and outcasts. In the reading from Luke we see him actually invite himself to stay the night at the home of Zacchaeus, the chief tax collector and, by accounts, a defrauder. The crowd is shocked that Jesus would do this. Nevertheless, the gospel narrative continues, and shows that Zacchaeus—outcast that he is—is also a good man. He tells Jesus, "Behold, Lord, the half of my goods I give to the poor; and if I have defrauded any one of any thing,

I restore it fourfold." It is surprising how much goodness there is in people we may feel threatened by, or dislike.

As Christians we have to struggle continually to live according to the call we receive from the Lord to be children of the kingdom. For Jesus, no man is "different," no woman an "outcast," no child an "outsider," no teenager a "stranger," no elderly person a "castoff." For Christians, there is no "our own kind," understood in any context of separation and aloofness, much less contempt of others. We need to remember that our religion was founded by a crucified Jew, propagated by Greeks, kept alive in dark ages by the Irish, theologized by the Germans and French, ruled by Italians, and brought to these shores by the wildest assortment of immigrants imaginable. As Christians, we, above all, are a universal people, and the openness of our minds and hearts should always be indicative of our basic belief in the unity of all peoples. We welcome outcasts by refusing to see them as such.

Reflect on your attitudes toward people different from you, especially those with different religious, political, or moral persuasions. How much tolerance and compassion do you have? Can you accept differences as God-given? Think of how different you appear to others; would they be wrong in treating you as an outcast? Love allows you to see beneath the surface of people—this was the great talent of Jesus. Allow your love to see goodness in everyone.

THIRTY-SECOND SUNDAY IN ORDINARY TIME
2 Maccabees 7:1–2, 9–14 2 Thessalonians 2:16–3:5 **Luke 20:27–38**

GOD OF THE LIVING

In Jesus' time, the Sadducees were an influential religious sect. They claimed belief in God but did not believe that individuals survived after death. The gospel reading of Luke suggests that Jesus' affirming views on life after death were well known to his followers. In the narrative, it is likely that Jesus had been preaching about life after death. The Sadducees were trying to bait him, and make fun of him, with the question about the widow with seven husbands. If a widow was married seven times during her lifetime, to whom would she end up being married in an afterlife? Jesus answers that, after death, there is no marriage and, therefore, the question is pointless. But Jesus goes on and, in one of his clearest affirmations of an afterlife, proclaims "that the dead are raised." As Christians we accept the Lord at his word, and trust that we will rise to eternal life after we pass from this world. But sometimes this trust is challenged. In moments of spiritual dryness, grief, or despair, we may be tempted to doubt our immortality, or that of others. After all, we have no direct experience of an afterlife. No one comes back to tell us what it is like on "the other side." We hear stories of people who have had a near death experience and live to tell that they journeyed to a place of intense light and love. But can we believe these stories? Could they be fantasies? Is there any substantiation that Jesus offers to encourage us that we will indeed be raised?

Jesus does offer substantiation for his affirmation, and it is also revealed in the gospel reading. In speaking of God, Jesus says: "Now he is not God of the dead, but of the living; for all live to him." The emphasis here is not on some claim we mortal creatures have on immortality, but on the nature of God. God is a living God, a God of the living. God's life is the one life that pours life into everything that lives. We have no life on our own; we cannot claim to have independently originated our own

existence. We live because God shares life with us. This, therefore, is the reason for our expectation that we will be raised
upon our death: our life is ultimately divine life, a life that cannot but be eternal. God's life, which is our very being, cannot
die. As long as God lives, we live.

We need to ponder this great truth about ourselves more
often. Our life is not animal life, or merely human life, it is
divine. The Spirit of God energizes the entire universe, but
nowhere more evidently than in conscious human beings.
Among all God's creation, we are unique because we can reflect
upon ourselves, and, therefore, come to know our true origin,
our true inner nature. We know ourselves as immortal when we
know ourselves as divine. Our God is a God of the living, and
we live "to" God, Jesus says. Sharing God's life guarantees that
we will be "raised."

> One of the most important, and rewarding, reflections you
> can make is about your spiritual nature. Spend some time
> reflecting on who you are. Enhance your life every day by
> pondering that your life shares God's life. Place your hope
> for immortality, not on fears your ego has over extinction,
> but on an understanding of your true inner being. Sharing
> God's life, you live eternally as God lives eternally. It is all
> one life! Take heart and joy that the one life you share from
> God makes you immortal.

FAITHFULNESS

In the gospel reading, Jesus speaks about the future and portents of things to come. He describes destruction, wars, famines, pestilences, and persecution that his followers will experience. By any accounts, it's a frightening picture. Furthermore, in times of turmoil, Jesus predicts, many claimants will come forward offering their prescriptions for salvation. He bids his disciples: "Do not go after them." In many respects, do not these dire predictions of Jesus reflect the experience of our own times? Times are uncertain. News reports are consistently bad. Major war seems to be on hold, but conflicts continue all over the globe with wanton destruction of life and property. Ethnic groups are persecuted almost everywhere. Not a year goes by without some nation experiencing famine and pestilence. And, true to the mark, never before have so many claimants come forward with a variety of formulas for happy and effective living; the market is glutted with "experts." As Christians we cannot help but be affected by the times we live in. How are we to react? The encouragement Jesus offers is the same he gave to his first disciples. He comforts us with assurance that God will always be with us and that, "not a hair of your head will perish." For our part, Jesus also promises: "By your endurance you will gain your lives." Endurance! What will save us, Jesus affirms, is our faithfulness.

In rapidly changing times, however, faithfulness is not easy to come by, much less practice. Our "throwaway" culture doesn't encourage permanence of any kind. Friends and acquaintances, for example, come and go, even spouses. According to forecasts, young people currently entering the job market will change jobs four or five times over a lifetime. The political climate alternates with every new crisis. Even our beliefs about what is important in life have a tendency to keep shifting. Through all this Jesus encourages faithfulness. But what kind of faithfulness is possible? And faithfulness to what? The answer in Jesus' exhortation is implicit: faithfulness is remaining true to our life's *purpose*. Times will always be difficult; society will always have its problems. People will continue to come and go in our lives; tastes and appetites will vary; interests and opinions will change. We may pursue new careers and explore different life-styles. Whatever the shifting events and moods of life, Jesus teaches us that our true purpose for living is to love, and that faithfulness to love is the one permanent foundation for secure, fulfilled, and happy living. As long as we love, we have nothing to fear, no matter what turmoil we experience. Even for finding success in life, faithfulness to love is all we need pursue. As Mother Teresa is fond of reminding us, "God calls us not to success, but to faithfulness." With respect to success, faithfulness proves to be its own reward.

In all of life's changes and turmoil, maintain your stability and a firm sense of identity by anchoring your life to something unshakeable. Anchor your life in fidelity to the Lord and his way of life. Faithfulness to being a loving person gives your life all the meaning and purpose it needs. Don't permit "trying times," bad news, shifting public opinion, economic uncertainties, or personal hardships to destroy your equilibrium and peace of mind. In moments of despair or confusion, always remember what you are for. You have no need to be frightened, no matter how chaotic the times may be, as long as you remain true to your purpose. Trust that in God's care, "not a hair of your head will perish," and continue to live by love.

PAY ATTENTION

Thanksgiving is an important feast day and should never be taken for granted as just another holiday. As we gather with family and friends, we not only enjoy good companionship and fine eating, we are reminded of our need to be grateful. "Thank you" can easily become so perfunctory that it loses its emotive edge. It is difficult to reflect honestly on all the things we enjoy in life, even life itself, without feeling passionate about "thank you." And so we reflect today on the bounties of our family, our material possessions, our talents and achievements, the people who have come into our lives, the happy experiences life has given us to enjoy, even the painful experiences that have taught us invaluable lessons. We already have had a full share of life's blessings and know that even more are on the way. It stands to reason, therefore, that we not only be grateful but that we show gratitude.

It is often said that we show gratitude best by using well the gifts God has given us. True enough. We can also show how thankful we are by returning favor for favor. If we have been blessed, for example, with financial abundance, we can demonstrate thankfulness by being generous with our means. Being of service to others is another admirable way to express thankfulness. But there is a way of showing gratitude, especially to people who are important to us, that isn't often given the consideration it deserves. Gratitude can be expressed in giving graciously of ourselves to others, and this can best be done by responding to their needs. But we cannot respond to someone's needs unless we are clearly *aware* of them. For example, many sincere and hardworking parents may give their children "the best that money can buy," without realizing that what their children really need from them is more loving attention.

The best way we might show gratitude, therefore, is to *pay attention*. And we need to realize that paying attention most often requires discipline. To really pay attention to others means we look at them deeply, and listen to them thoroughly. Let us not imagine this kind of discipline comes to us easily. We tend to judge a book by its cover. We look at the surface of people's personalities and rarely inquire if we are perceiving the real person within, or what's really going on in their lives. It takes effort to notice. What can we say, for example, about a parent who comments, "I just noticed that my little girl is all grown up." We might wonder where attention has been all these years. Listening is not automatic either. We often think we know what others need better than they do, and impose our own needs without really listening to them at all. Countless arguments go on in the average household because we don't make the effort to understand where another family member is really coming from. Even in casual conversation, we generally only half-listen to what someone else is saying. It's not that we're trying to be mean, only that we're anxious to get our point across and are, therefore, paying more attention to ourselves. Gratitude, therefore, is turning outward in awareness of where other people are coming from. The lesson of Thanksgiving is: "pay attention."

> Look at the people you love. What do you see? How truly aware are you of the most important people in your life as individual persons with their own identities, personality makeups, and needs? Gratitude is demonstrated in a loving response to the needs of others. What do the people you love need most from you, individually? Listen carefully. Pay close attention to what others are trying to say. If it feels like an effort, it's working.

SHIFT AT CENTER

The feast of Christ the King is associated with majestic imagery. Christian art depicts the son of God, arrayed in glory, worshiped by heavenly hosts, and sitting in regal judgment over all mankind. We don't begrudge Jesus his triumph, nor do we insinuate he is not worthy of highest acclaim. The imagery, however, is certainly a far cry from the humble Nazarene whose footsteps we trace in the gospels, and especially from the Jesus we see on the cross in the reading today from Luke. The problem with the imagery of Christ in imperial splendor is that it can divert us from consideration of the intimate place the Lord should have in our hearts. Enthroned in glory, Jesus appears distant, aloof, and far removed from the affairs of our everyday life. Yet, we know from the gospels, this is not the desire of Jesus at all. There are many references in the gospels of the promise of Jesus to be with us, to "dwell" within us, to be intimately connected with us as a vine is connected with its branches. We need to examine, therefore, another interpretation of the kingship of Jesus.

One great mark of a Christian is a conversion experience that leads one to confess that "Jesus is the Lord." This confession not only acknowledges Jesus' prominence in all creation, but accepts Jesus into a new position in our lives. All of us are aware that our lives are "run" by all manner of desires, fears, worries, threats, beliefs, and experiences from our past. All put together, these pressures are what constitute our self-consciousness, our self, our ego. The ego tries to rule us with omnipotent pretensions. The primary agenda of the ego is to persuade us to identify exclusively with its needs, to make us believe that we cannot exist without it. It sets about its daily business with one objective in mind: "my will be done." In confessing Jesus as "Lord," however, we remove ego from the throne of our hearts and give this position of eminence over to Jesus Christ. In making this confession, we actually become a new creation, a new person, "born again." This doesn't mean we become sinless, or perfect, or without problems, only that something substantial has shifted within us. Christ has become our *center*. With Christ as our center, we surrender to a higher power, a new controlling force, to "run" our lives.

This shift is of such magnitude, and has such enormous repercussions for the way we live, that we can never treat it lightly. The shift, rightly called "salvation," does not destroy the ego, but saves us from ego-centricity. The ego is displaced; its central position at the controls of our life is converted to the Lord; it is from Christ that we now have a new self-consciousness. This conversion is reflected in an attitude of "Thy will be done," an intention to live from the mind of Christ, and a willingness to take our cues for effective living from the teachings of Jesus. Christ lives then, not only as King of the universe, but as ruler of our hearts.

What "runs" your life? Are you aware of what power your ego has over you, of how it operates, and how much conflict and suffering it often brings into your life? How much has your ego already drawn you away from your true spiritual Self? Are you perhaps ready for a shift at your center, a conversion that surrenders your ego's rule for Christ's dominion? Affirm Jesus as "Lord" of your life. Plan your life, change your life-style, make decisions, and act from the mind of Christ. See if your life doesn't substantially improve with a new self-consciousness: a loving Christ the King at the center of your heart.

TOPICS AND THEMES
(O.T.= Ordinary Time)

ACCEPTING AFFIRMATION
Ascension

ACCOUNTABILITY
Twenty-Sixth Sunday in O.T.

ADULT CHRISTIANITY
Fourteenth Sunday in O.T.

ADULTHOOD
Fourth Sunday in O.T.

ATTACHMENT
Twenty-Third Sunday in O.T.
Christ the King

AWARENESS
Second Sunday of Lent
The Body and Blood of
Christ

BEATITUDES
Sixth Sunday in O.T.

BLESSINGS IN DISGUISE
Sixth Sunday in O.T.

BORN AGAIN
Christ the King

CHANGE
Second Sunday of Advent
Third Sunday of Easter

CHANGING OTHERS
Twenty-Fourth Sunday in
O.T.

CHRISTIAN LIFE-STYLE
Seventh Sunday in O.T.

CHRISTIAN VOCATION
Fourth Sunday of Easter

The Body and Blood of
Christ
Twentieth Sunday in O.T.
Assumption of the Virgin
Mary
Christ the King

CHRISTIAN COMMUNITY
Holy Thursday
Seventh Sunday of Easter
Third Sunday in O.T.
Ninth Sunday in O.T.
Thirty-First Sunday in O.T.

COMMITMENT
Thirteenth Sunday in O.T.
Twenty-Ninth Sunday in
O.T.

COMMON GOOD
Third Sunday in O.T.

COMPASSION
Fifth Sunday of Lent
Good Friday
Ninth Sunday in O.T.
Thirty-First Sunday in O.T.

CONFIDENCE
Easter

CONQUERING EVIL
Good Friday

CONSUMERISM
Eighteenth Sunday in O.T.

DEATH
Tenth Sunday in O.T.
All the Faithful Departed
(All Souls)
Thirty-Second Sunday in
O.T.

EFFECTIVE LIVING
Baptism of the Lord
First Sunday of Lent
Good Friday
Third Sunday of Easter
Fifth Sunday of Easter
Sixth Sunday of Easter
Ascension
Pentecost
Second Sunday in O.T.
Fifth Sunday in O.T.
Thirteenth Sunday in O.T.
Seventeenth Sunday in O.T.
Thirty-Third Sunday in O.T.

EGO
Twelfth Sunday in O.T.
Christ the King

EMPOWERMENT
Passion (Palm) Sunday
Twenty-Seventh Sunday in
O.T.

ENTHUSIASM
Twenty-Seventh Sunday in
O.T.

ENVY
Second Sunday in O.T.

ENTHUSIASM
Pentecost

EXCELLENCE
Epiphany
Fifth Sunday of Easter
Ascension

FAITH
Second Sunday of Easter
Fourth Sunday of Easter
Fourteenth Sunday in O.T.
Nineteenth Sunday in O.T.
Twentieth Sunday in O.T.

FAITHFULNESS
Thirty-Third Sunday in O.T.

FAMILY LIFE
Holy Family

FEAR
Nineteenth Sunday in O.T.

FINDING GOD
Second Sunday of Lent

FORGIVENESS
Fourth Sunday of Lent
Good Friday
Twenty-Fourth Sunday in
O.T.

FORGIVENESS OF SIN
Eleventh Sunday in O.T.

GENEROSITY
Twenty-Third Sunday in
O.T.

GOD
Solemnity of the Holy
Trinity

GOD'S PRESENCE
All Saints

GOD'S WILL
Fourth Sunday of Advent
Thirtieth Sunday in O.T.

GRACE
Third Sunday of Lent
Assumption of the Virgin
Mary

GRACIOUSNESS
Solemnity of Mary,
Mother of God (New
Year's Day)

GRATITUDE
Thanksgiving

HOLINESS
All Saints

HOPE
Easter

HUMILITY
Twenty-Second Sunday in
O.T.

HOSPITALITY
Solemnity of Mary,
Mother of God (New
Year's Day)

HYPOCRISY
Fifth Sunday of Lent

JOY
Third Sunday of Advent

JOYFUL LIVING
Third Sunday of Advent

JUDGING OTHERS
Fifth Sunday of Lent
Eighth Sunday in O.T.

JUSTIFICATION
Eleventh Sunday in O.T.

LAW
Eleventh Sunday in O.T.

LEARNING FROM MISTAKES
Third Sunday of Lent

LIFE
Tenth Sunday in O.T.
The Body and Blood of
Christ
Thirty-Second Sunday in
O.T.

LIFE AFTER DEATH
Thirty-Second Sunday in
O.T.

LITTLE THINGS COUNT
Twenty-Fifth Sunday in O.T.

LIVING IN THE PRESENT
Ash Wednesday

LORDSHIP OF JESUS
First Sunday of Lent
Christ the King

LOVE
Fifth Sunday of Easter
Fourth Sunday in O.T.
Seventh Sunday in O.T.
Eleventh Sunday in O.T.
Twenty-Third Sunday in O.T.
Twenty-Fourth Sunday in
O.T.
Twenty-Fifth Sunday in O.T.
Thirty-First Sunday in O.T.
Thanksgiving

MARRIAGE
Fourteenth Sunday in O.T.
Twenty-Ninth Sunday in
O.T.

MATERIALISM
Eighteenth Sunday in O.T.

MEANING IN LIFE
All the Faithful Departed (All
Souls)

MINISTRY
Fourth Sunday of Easter

NAME OF JESUS
Passion (Palm) Sunday

PARISH LIFE
Holy Thursday
Fourth Sunday of Easter
Fifth Sunday of Easter
Seventh Sunday of Easter

PEACE OF MIND
Fourth Sunday of Lent
Good Friday

PERSEVERANCE
Twenty-Ninth Sunday in O.T.

137

POSSESSIONS
Twenty-Third Sunday in O.T.

PRAYER
Sixth Sunday of Easter
Seventeenth Sunday in O.T.
Twenty-Ninth Sunday in
O.T.
Thirtieth Sunday in O.T.

PRESENCE OF GOD
Sixth Sunday of Easter

PRIDE
Twenty-Second Sunday in
O.T.

PRIMACY OF CHRIST
Christ the King

PRIORITIES
Sixteenth Sunday in O.T.
All the Faithful Departed (All
Souls)

PROBLEM-SOLVING
Seventeenth Sunday in O.T.

PROCRASTINATION
Ash Wednesday

PURPOSE OF LIFE
Epiphany
Fifth Sunday of Easter
Thirty-Third Sunday in O.T.

RELATIONSHIPS
Seventh Sunday of Easter
Thanksgiving

RELIGION
Twentieth Sunday in O.T.

RESENTMENT
Fourth Sunday of Lent
Good Friday

RESOURCES
Baptism of the Lord

RESPONSIBILITY
Thirteenth Sunday in O.T.

RIGHTEOUSNESS
First Sunday of Advent

SALVATION
Passion (Palm) Sunday

SELF-DEVELOPMENT
First Sunday of Advent
Epiphany

SELF-ESTEEM
Ascension

SELF-HELP
Seventeenth Sunday in O.T.

SELF-KNOWLEDGE
Eighth Sunday in O.T.

SELF-RIGHTEOUSNESS
Fifth Sunday of Lent

SPIRIT
Baptism of the Lord
Sixth Sunday of Easter
Pentecost
Twelfth Sunday in O.T.
Twenty-Seventh Sunday in
O.T.
Thirty-Second Sunday in
O.T.

SPIRITUAL LIFE/GROWTH
First Sunday of Advent
Second Sunday of Advent
Third Sunday of Advent
Christmas
Second Sunday of Lent
Second Sunday of Easter
Fifth Sunday of Easter
Ascension
Seventh Sunday of Easter
Pentecost
Sixteenth Sunday in O.T.
Eighteenth Sunday in O.T.

SUCCESS
Thirty-Third Sunday in O.T.

SUFFERING, MEANING OF
Easter
Sixth Sunday in O.T.

SURRENDER
Twelfth Sunday in O.T.

TRANSFIGURATION
Second Sunday of Lent

VANITY OF VANITIES
Eighteenth Sunday in O.T.

WILLPOWER
Twenty-Sixth Sunday in O.T.

Weekday Reflections
for Lent

INTRODUCTION

This section presents lessons in personal growth based on the liturgical readings for the weekdays of Lent. It offers reflections for spiritual development during this special season of the church year. The Scripture readings assigned for each weekday have been examined for one specific insight that could be instrumental in improving the quality of one's life.

These reflections are offered to anyone looking upon Lent as an important time for change and development, and willing to use the inexhaustible richness of the Word of the Lord as a resource for more effective and bountiful living. They can be useful to preachers as a source of seminal ideas for daily homilies and days of recollection, to Bible study groups searching for ways to make Scripture come "alive," and also to editors for relevant essay material for parish bulletins and other publications.

STARTING FROM ASHES

Lent is traditionally a special time of the church year in which we are encouraged to perform an in-depth evaluation of where we are going with our lives, especially in terms of our Christian values. Time is set aside for contemplation of our mortality and for repentance of our sins, but also for an assessment of our potential as spiritual beings, made in the image and likeness of God. We examine where we're falling behind in our spiritual growth and make fresh resolves to carry on in our Christian calling with renewed vigor and enthusiasm. The mood is somber, yet full of promise. It is a journey from ashes to Easter.

It is fitting that Lent begin with ashes. Ashes have a way of putting things in perspective. When we receive ashes, we are encouraged to see ourselves in the light of our mortality. Ashes demonstrate the folly of human vanity and the implausibility of possessions to give us what we need to be happy in life. Ashes also confront any smugness or undue self-assurance we might have in our material well-being, and remind us of our need to develop spiritually. We are assured that we have much yet to do to fulfill our true purpose in life and that the journey must continue.

There is no better time than the present to consider that journey, and how we are making it. In today's reading from Corinthians, Paul states: "now is the acceptable time; behold now is the day of salvation." NOW is the acceptable time to challenge our apathy, evaluate our present life-style, and reorganize our priorities. God has special graces for us this lenten season and beckons us to clarify our vision of what we are about as followers of the Lord Jesus. It is up to us to take advantage of the moment, and accept these graces. We don't have to wait for salvation, it is available for us right now.

Promise to keep Lent special, and take advantage of its special graces. Dedicate this Lent to your personal growth.

Are you willing to devote these forty days to review where you are in life, and where God wants to lead you? Receive ashes with humility, and be willing to learn. Look forward to Easter as a time you will feel raised from the dead with new awareness and vigor for your spiritual journey. The Word of the Lord is ready to show you the way. Begin now!

THURSDAY AFTER ASH WEDNESDAY
Deuteronomy 30:15–20   Luke 9:22–25

CHOOSE LIFE

Something we easily observe about life is that it is a remarkable composite of opposites: darkness and light, cold and hot, sour and sweet, pain and pleasure, suffering and bliss, bad and good, failure and promise, stops and starts, death and birth. While there is nothing we can do to change life's polarities, we are remarkably free to determine on which side of those polarities we wish to live. For example, we can choose good habits over bad habits, self-responsibility over self-pity, and enthusiasm over laziness, as ways of handling our life. The choice is up to us, and we make or break our life by the choices we make.

In the reading from Deuteronomy, God speaks through Moses and offers an ultimatum: death or life; death-dealing ways of living or life-enhancing ways of living. God implores us to choose life. At first glance, we may believe there is no real choice in the matter; of course we want to choose life. But do we? We need to reflect on some of our basic attitudes. Do we tend to see the dark side of people and situations rather than the bright, faults rather than assets, setbacks rather than opportunities, something to criticize rather than praise? Has growing up soured us so that our days are full of complaint rather than gratitude? How many of us take too much too seriously and have lost the ability to laugh at our pretensions? Let there be no doubt about it, these are life and death choices. There is a life and death choice even in the gospel reading from Luke, where

Jesus encourages us to take up our cross and follow him. Taking up a cross doesn't seem very life-enhancing, but it is. It's important to note that Jesus doesn't say we should lay down our crosses, or sit with them, or pass them on to others, but that we *carry* them with our eyes glued on the Lord. What this means is that we don't deny our problems, or resign ourselves to them, or blame other people for them, but that we *deal* with them courageously in the light of the teachings of Jesus. Dealing with problems as we need to is clearly an example of a life-enhancing choice.

> Among all life's opposites and polarities, choose what enhances your life. See good in people rather than evil. Hunt for the good in yourself, rather than lamenting your weaknesses and failings. Focus on the light rather than the darkness, the sweet rather than the sour, successes rather than defeats, support rather than criticism, gratefulness rather than complaint. The choice of life over death is yours to make.

FRIDAY AFTER ASH WEDNESDAY
Isaiah 58:1–9a Matthew 9:14–15

MORE THAN GIVING UP TREATS

Most people believe religion should be kept private, that religious practices should be personal and self-directed. This may be reflected in the way we keep Lent. Lent is traditionally a penitential season, a time for mortification, penance, and fasting. Perhaps from childhood we have used Lent to impose acts of self-discipline upon ourselves; in the spirit of the season we give up something. Our practice of Lent, therefore, also tends to be a private affair, and we may think that we are keeping Lent well because we fast from certain treats.

In today's reading, however, the prophet Isaiah interprets "fasting" from a different perspective. There is nothing self-directed, personal, or private about it at all. "Is not this the fast that I choose: to loose the bonds of wickedness, to undo the thongs of the yoke, to let the oppressed go free, and to break every yoke? Is it not to share your bread with the hungry, and bring the homeless into your house; when you see the naked, to cover him, and not hide from your own flesh?" Hearing God speak through his mighty prophet, we are challenged to broaden our ideas about fasting and giving up something for Lent. We are not discouraged from personal penances, but God turns our eyes toward bigger issues in our lives that are in need of penance. Of what use is giving up ice cream for Lent if our relationship with a spouse, a neighbor, or a coworker is strained under a "yoke" of neglect or abusive treatment? Are we practicing Lent by abstaining from smoking when we "oppress" members of our family with biting criticism or caustic remarks? Will giving up chocolate help us grow spiritually when we are "yoked" to demands that we always have our way? Do our hearts go out to the hungry and homeless, and do we look upon our unfortunate brothers and sisters in this world as part of our own "flesh"? There is more to penance than giving up pleasures for Lent. God calls us to conversion, a change of heart.

> Choose lenten practices in the light of God's expectations. Give up an abusive tongue or some mannerism that offends others. Break the "yoke" of a bad habit that is harming your health. "Free" someone from your criticism or lack of forgiveness. "Loose the bonds of wickedness," by capitalizing on your capacities for doing good. Be generous with your possessions. Is there any way you can help feed the hungry, or find shelter for the homeless? Rather than giving up a treat for Lent, consider giving more of yourself to others.

SATURDAY AFTER ASH WEDNESDAY
Isaiah 58:9–14 **Luke 5:27–32**

GOOD NEWS FOR SINNERS

Many people give up on themselves and the Christian way of

life because they are keenly aware of their sinfulness. Some are so sensitive to their faults and failings that they feel, "I can't do anything right," or, "I'm a failure." Maybe we don't despair that God still loves us, but we may feel that being a close follower of Christ is beyond serious consideration. Explicitly or implicitly, we may feel Jesus is too good for us. What a relief, then, to hear Jesus' assertion in the gospel reading that his mission is to *sinners* rather than the righteous. "Those who are well have no need of a physician, but those who are sick." In other words, it is the company of "sinners" that Jesus most avidly welcomes.

It is important that we take these words of the Lord to heart. It is precisely when we suffer and are afflicted with problems that Jesus is most ready to be at our side. It is when we become sensitive to our failings, and feel the weight of our guilt, that he is most available with support and healing. When we fall, no matter how seriously, and no matter how many times, the Lord is anxious to help us up. And the reason for this should be obvious. When we appreciate our mistakes and acknowledge our failings, we are at our most humble. This is exactly what opens for us the door to grace. It is when we are aware of illness that we become ready for treatment.

> Your sensitivity to your sinfulness is an asset, not a liability, to the Christian way of life. Never let it make you feel that you are "unworthy" of Christ. Turn to the Lord, therefore, when you feel most down on yourself. Pray to him especially when you see yourself in the darkest light. The teachings of Jesus will never make more sense than when you are burdened with confusion and self-doubt. There is no better time to follow the Lord than when you find yourself taking all the wrong roads in life. He "who takes away the sins of the world" wishes to take away yours, whenever you're ready to permit him. Jesus doesn't do this with reluctance; it is precisely what he is all about! Jesus best reveals himself as "savior," when he is actually saving you.

GOD TAKES IT PERSONALLY

We generally tend to see ourselves as good or bad in reference to how God might see us. We consider our sins as offenses against God. When we are repentant, we ask God's forgiveness. We want to die in grace so that God will reward us with eternal happiness in heaven, and we accept the message of Jesus, in today's gospel reading from Matthew, that a final judgment one day awaits us all. However, we miss an important point in this gospel passage if we too quickly pass over an intriguing revelation about God's judgment of us. True, Jesus is presented as a final judge of our actions but we also learn something about how Jesus identifies himself as a judge. Jesus identifies himself with ordinary people. "Truly, I say to you, as you did it to one of the least of these my brethren, you did it to me," and "truly, as you did it not to one of the least of these, you did it not to me." What this identification does is prevent us from escaping responsibility to the people whose lives we touch. It suggests that our consciences be directed, not so much to God abiding in a world beyond, but to a very mundane, earthy, and practical world where real people live.

What this gospel passage indicates is that our moral status is never just "between me and God." What we do, or don't do, for others is what counts in the eyes of the Lord. We can pray fervently to God and yet be poor communicators to members of our own family. We can be repentant to God for our sins and be unrepentant to those whom we have actually offended. We can dutifully fulfill our religious obligations and yet be neglectful of our responsibilities for the poor and downtrodden in society. Not offering a helping hand where it is needed, not giving good example to our children, "keeping our nose clean" when our input could be useful, turning our back on someone in trouble, refusing a request for forgiveness—all these, and more, God takes very personally.

Set your eyes directly on those affected by your actions or neglect. Don't approach God for forgiveness without first taking "the least of these my brethren" into account. Praise God by praising the efforts of your children. Glorify God by rejoicing with your neighbors in their good fortune. Seek God's forgiveness by seeking forgiveness of people you actually hurt. Thank God by expressing gratitude to people who have shown you kindness. Show God love by the love you offer to those who need it most.

TUESDAY OF THE FIRST WEEK OF LENT
Isaiah 55:10–11 **Matthew 6:7–15**

A DANGEROUS PRAYER

One of the most common prayers we recite is The Lord's Prayer. In Matthew's account, Jesus encourages his disciples not to ramble on in long, wordy prayers. He offers them a simple prayer that addresses the most important needs in life. In this prayer, God is praised, God's will is acknowledged, material sustenance and forgiveness for sin are requested, and a plea is made for God's protection against harm. A peculiar twist, however, can be noted in a part of this simple. God is requested to forgive us *as* we forgive others. In other words, we beseech God to be willing to forgive us in proportion to our willingness to forgive others. It is a stark bargain, but a bargain nevertheless. Jesus confirms this with a warning at the conclusion of the gospel passage: "For if you forgive men their trespasses, your heavenly Father also will forgive you; but if you do not forgive men their trespasses, neither will your Father forgive your trespasses."

We might wonder, therefore, when we frequently and casually offer this prayer, how alert we are that we are calling down upon ourselves either a blessing or a curse. In terms of offering God the conditions for our forgiveness, this is a dangerous prayer. If we are free and open with our forgiveness of others, of course, we have little to fear when we give God this challenge. If, on the other hand, we are resentful, peevish, eager for revenge, and reluctant with our forgiveness of others, we stand on precarious ground. Either we stop saying this prayer, or significantly change our attitudes on forgiveness.

Does forgiveness come to you easily? Do you bear grudges and resentments over years of time? Consider how much you may have harmed and hurt others over a lifetime. Wouldn't it be great relief to know that all is forgiven and forgotten, and that God would never hold it against you? That relief is as close as your willingness to forgive others. Say the Lord's Prayer with all sincerity of heart, but be alert to its implications. Commit yourself to be as forgiving as you can, and then you can trust God to return the favor.

WEDNESDAY OF THE FIRST WEEK OF LENT
Jonah 3:1–10   Luke 11:29–32

NECESSARY LOSSES

Any improvement in our life will require some kind of change. Change is always difficult for human beings, and what makes it difficult are the necessary losses involved in any change process. For marriage to be a success, for example, certain freedoms that a single person enjoys will have to be given up. But we don't like giving things up, even when we know they are bad for us. In efforts to avoid the pain of loss, we often compromise our values and try to accommodate the old with the new. We look forward, for instance, to the promised land, but, like the ancient Hebrews in their desert wanderings, we long for the "fleshpots" of the city left behind. Which, of course, leads to problems. Hanging on to the old with the new means we operate at cross purposes, and often with dire consequences. A college graduate, for example, who tries to bring dorm life into the business world will seriously jeopardize his career plans. The alcoholic who believes he can handle drinking again after months of sobriety is in for terrible surprise.

Most of us fail to achieve a better and happier life for our-selves, not for lack of desire, but because we hang on to so much from the past. In the reading from Jonah, the prophet is sent to the city of Nineveh to convert it. For God, there was no com-promise with certain values. God relents on destroying the inhabitants only when they "turn away" from their evil ways. There may be certain areas in our lives where we need to turn away from an old life-style with no compromises and no look-ing back. We may have certain habits that should no longer be accommodated in any way. There should be no accommodation whatever, for example, for self-destructive addictions, for atti-tudes and behaviors that hurt the people we say we love, or for a style of living that stifles our spiritual growth.

What is holding you back from living more effectively? What prevents you from attaining the happiness you so eagerly desire? Is it laziness, procrastination, your tenden-cy to lie to yourself or deny your talents, your lack of sta-mina in keeping your resolutions? Are you in the habit of being harsh, demanding, critical, and one-sided in the way you handle other people, especially those you love? All of us have anchors that bind us to unproductive living. What are yours, and are you willing to muster the courage to let them go once and for all?

THURSDAY OF THE FIRST WEEK OF LENT
Esther 14:1, 3–5, 12–15a Matthew 7:7–12

ASK FOR WHAT YOU NEED

Marriages, friendships, even work situations run into serious trouble when people in a relationship begin assuming their counterparts have the power to read minds. Many of us are hes-itant to express our needs out of fear of showing weakness or vulnerability. But we also assume that our needs should be "obvious" to the people we care about, and remain reluctant to speak about them openly. We believe, for example, that others should be able to guess why we are pouting. When our needs are not automatically recognized, we then assume that our partners don't care about us or are deliberately trying to hurt us.

While there is no question that self-sufficiency is a valuable asset, we do ourselves a great disfavor by denying the times that we need something from others. We are social animals who, by nature, need one another to accomplish what we need to do to take care of ourselves. We are not meant to go it alone. We have needs, big ones and small ones, of which there is no reason to feel ashamed, because this is what being human is all about. Nor should there be any shame or reluctance in *expressing* those needs. In the gospel reading from Matthew, Jesus makes this clear: "Ask, and it will be given to you; seek, and you will find; knock, and it will be opened to you." What Jesus advocates is a proactive approach to having our needs met. That we acknowledge what we need and then *go after* it. That we don't sit back and wait for things to happen, or expect other people to read our minds about what we need. If there is something we need to sustain our well-being, or increase our peace, hope, motivation, joy, even physical and emotional satisfaction, it is up to us to ask, seek, and knock.

> Are there certain needs in your life that you believe other people *should* be aware of without you expressing them? Do you become irritated and blaming when your needs are not met, even though you never openly talk about them? Hinting doesn't count. If there is something you need, you should be able to express it, be it to God, family members, a friend, a teacher, an employer, or anyone who can help you. Why should you be reluctant to appear vulnerable to people you care about? Put shame aside, therefore, and stop being afraid to appear human. Don't expect others to be mind-readers. Tell people where you are hurting; let others clearly know what you need from them. Only those who ask, receive.

RIGHTEOUSNESS

In the gospel narrative of Matthew, Jesus admonishes his disciples that they will never enter the kingdom "unless your righteousness exceeds that of the scribes and Pharisees." What kind of "righteousness" is Jesus talking about, and how must it "exceed"? For one thing, we know the Pharisees were sticklers for legalities; right living was obeying the law down to its finest points. But this wasn't enough for kingdom living as far as Jesus was concerned. In this passage from Matthew, Jesus demonstrates a righteousness that does exceed that of the scribes and Pharisees. It is a righteousness, or right living, that does not dismiss or discount the law, but transcends it in its expectations. It isn't enough, for example, not to kill another human being, there should be no place for insults and other forms of abuse. Rituals in God's honor can be put temporarily aside if we need to reconcile ourselves with neighbors with whom we are at odds. It is better to amicably settle disputes without resorting to lawsuits. What these examples suggest is that entering the kingdom requires an attitude of heart that goes beyond legalities.

Attitudes say more about us than our behaviors; where we're coming from reveals our character more than what we say or do. Behavior stems from our attitudes. If, for example, we implicitly believe that people exist to serve us, we will treat them condescendingly and try to manipulate them to do what we want. If, on the other hand, we are basically loving, we will generally act in a loving manner toward others without any need for "legislation." A man, for example, who truly loves his wife doesn't need a rule book to tell him to care for her, treat her nicely, and buy her presents now and then—he does it automatically on his own.

Are you a stickler for "the rules" even when some higher consideration is being called for? Can you withhold criticism if you see it will do more harm than good? If you were in an accident, would your first thoughts be about people being hurt, or about lawsuits? Are you more concerned with "facts," rather than people's inner feelings? Do you hold back forgiveness until retribution is made to your exact specifications? Are you able to easily break routines and schedules to give someone a helping hand? Can you picture yourself living more from your heart than from regulations? The law looks toward your behavior, but the Lord looks toward your heart. Live the righteousness Jesus calls for by always acting, first and foremost, out of love.

SATURDAY OF THE FIRST WEEK OF LENT
Deuteronomy 26:16–19 Matthew 5:43–48

PERFECT AS GOD IS PERFECT

Both readings today offer us a formidable challenge. In the passage from Deuteronomy, Moses presents the people of God with God's commands and stipulates that God expects them to be "holy." Furthermore, in the reading from Matthew, Jesus admonishes his followers that they be "perfect" even as God is perfect. Is this possible? By any stretch of the imagination, are these expectations reasonable? As weak, finite and fault-ridden human beings, are we honestly capable of holiness? And isn't it completely unrealistic to believe we can be perfect as God is perfect?

We can be assured, however, that Moses and Jesus are not speaking pious rhetoric; the admonitions are urgent and clear. But so is the implication of how holiness and divine perfection become possible for us. Moses and Jesus teach us about God and how God operates. God chose the people of Israel out of love for them. Through Moses, God gives them commandments for their own well-being and the fulfillment of their destiny, which is to "walk in his ways" and reflect God's love to all nations. Jesus reveals God's perfection as a lover. In the reading from Matthew, Jesus instructs us to imitate God by making love our absolute rule of life—love for everybody, in every situation,

even to the point of loving our enemies and people who perse-
cute us. How is God perfect in love? God loves completely and
impartially; God, "makes his sun rise on the evil and the good,
and sends rain on the just and on the unjust." What Jesus
encourages is that we follow God's example in being just as
thorough, generous, and impartial with our own love. In this
way, we become perfect as God is perfect.

Become holy by adopting God's mind and ways of operating. It is in the way you *love* that you become perfect as
God is perfect. Holiness and perfection are not beyond
you, because you are made in God's image and likeness. It
is your destiny and purpose to mirror God's perfect love.
This is what spiritual growth is all about: becoming as loving as you can be. Don't believe this is an impossible task,
because love is your nature. Adopt the mind of God, therefore, in the way you look upon, and deal with, others. Be
perfect in treating all people in ways you would imagine
God treating them. Begin by eliminating partiality and
prejudice. See everyone as deserving of your love.

MONDAY OF THE SECOND WEEK OF LENT
Daniel 9:4b–10 **Luke 6:36–38**

IN LIKE MEASURE

It's a great feeling when things are going our way and we sense
a measure of control over our lives. It would be wonderful if
peace of mind, joy, and happiness could become permanent features of our day-to-day living. In today's gospel reading from
Luke, Jesus claims they can. While things will not always go our
way, and while there is no complete control over every situation
in our life, Jesus suggests something experience backs up: we
get out of life what we put into it. While there are certainly
exceptions, we generally get from life what we deserve. Give in
to laziness and we can expect poor achievement. Never try
something new and we stagnate. Keep a closed mind and we
remain ignorant. Hurt people and we likely get hurt back in

return. Steal and cheat and we are stolen from and cheated. Lie to people we care about and they feel free to lie back to us. On the other hand, as Jesus asserts, "judge not, and you will not be judged; condemn not, and you will not be condemned; forgive, and you will be forgiven; give, and it will be given to you." What Jesus affirms is borne out every day of our lives: "For the measure you give will be the measure you get back."

Very often, however, we forget the rule of "like measure." We expect more from life than we are willing to put in, or we fail to appreciate that all good things in life cost. Many people today, for example, expect something for nothing, and demand more money for less work. We may be hungry for love, but unconcerned about giving it. We may expect our friends to be there for us, but make excuses for not helping a friend who is in trouble. Most of us want to be understood and forgiven at the drop of a hat, and yet we rarely try to understand where other people are coming from, and may be obstinate in holding grudges. Jesus gives us both encouragement and warning: we get what we give.

> Take more mastery over your life with the rule of "like measure." Give what you hope to get. Fair treatment, peace of mind, love, joy, and happiness can be yours if this is what you yourself are about. Sow good seed, and you will likely reap a good harvest. Do favors, and favors will be returned. Be nice to people, and they will most often be nice to you. Make someone laugh, and you will laugh. Affirm others, and they will feel strength to affirm you. Make others happy, and you will be happy. Be a friend, and you will have friends. Give love, and you will receive it. "For the measure you give will be the measure you get back."

SHARING THE CREDIT

Jesus offers a warning to the proud and a promise to the humble in today's gospel reading from Matthew: "Whoever exalts himself will be humbled, and whoever humbles himself will be exalted." The encouragement for humility is clear enough, but not understanding "humility" correctly can impede our personal growth. Success breeds success. We are only human, and if we don't feel our efforts are paying off we tend to stop making them. Without pride in our achievements, we lose incentive to continue in our spiritual development. Many of us see humility as self-effacement or self-abnegation; we don't take credit for the good persons we are, or for the good that we do. We may be inclined to say: "oh, it was nothing," and be embarrassed by applause. Self-esteem, however, requires that we take genuine pride in ourselves and our achievements. God wishes us success and joy in the fullness of life. For Jesus, humility is not denying our worth as children of God, or putting ourselves down by disclaiming our accomplishments. Humility is pride suffused with gratitude; it is willingness to *share* the credit for what we do, with others.

The self-exaltation of which Jesus warns is *arrogance.* It is a claim to self-sufficiency that separates us from our essential connectedness with others. Arrogance is more than taking pride in our achievements, it's pretending we aren't indebted to others for what we accomplish in life. True humility is a willingness to gracefully share the credit for our achievements with God and others. It is acknowledging that we stand on the shoulders of others in our journey of life and that we make that journey with a lot of help from other people.

Never put yourself down by declining applause for the good things you do. You only harm your self-esteem by deflecting an affirmation with a disclaimer. Graciously accept compliments with a "thank you." At the same time, beware of arrogance. Think of the people without whom you could not sustain your life. Consider the food you eat, the clothes you wear, the knowledge you have, the love that sustains you, the opportunities for advancement you have been handed, and the like, and be grateful. Take healthy pride in your achievements; you deserve to. But be willing to share some of the credit with others. You will be "exalted" as you are willing to give recognition where recognition is due.

WEDNESDAY OF THE SECOND WEEK OF LENT
Jeremiah 18:18–20 **Matthew 20:17–28**

TO BE OF SERVICE

Ask ten people what it means to be a "good" Christian and we will likely get ten different answers. All of us have pet ideas of what constitutes an ideal follower of Christ. We may pride ourselves, for example, on keeping the Commandments, on our regular church attendance, prayer life, and generosity to the collection plate. We may attend Bible study classes, read good spiritual literature, and have religious articles prominently displayed in our homes. While all this is well and good, we may not be as attentive to a deeper dimension of the Christian way of life that is clear in the gospels. When Jesus invites us to follow him, he calls us not only to believe in him as the Way, the Truth, and the Life, but to continue his mission. And, as we can see from the reading of Matthew, that mission is one of service.

Jesus states: "... the Son of Man came not to be served but to serve." In this gospel passage, Jesus makes known the Christian mission, and discourages ruling over people, making demands of others, or having people at our beck and call. Jesus' life was one of service. The gospels record many of his teachings, but give equal measure to the *deeds* he performed on other people's behalf. Jesus has been defined as "a man for others." Can anything less be expected of his disciples? Our inclination in evaluating ourselves as Christian is very often to consider our personal religious virtues rather than our orientation to be of service. While it is important that we grow in piety, it is just as important that we grow in our compassionate care of others, especially those who depend on us. Our practice of the Christian way of life should be modeled on Jesus. This means that we too are called to teach, heal, console, forgive, reconcile, and pour out our love wherever it is needed. A "mission" means that we take an active role to be of service.

Are you willing to accept Jesus' definition of the Christian way of life, and commit yourself to being a "good" Christian in the way you serve the needs of others? Countless opportunities surround you on all sides, every day, to follow Christ in his mission. Is there someone in your family who needs your special attention, a friend who would appreciate a call? Are there people at work who could use a word of encouragement, a compliment, or some good advice? Can your parish or community use some talent or skill you have? Your power for doing good is beyond measure, and the Lord encourages you to use that power freely.

THURSDAY OF THE SECOND WEEK OF LENT
Jeremiah 17:5–10 Luke 16:19–31

LOWER YOUR DEFENSES

Both readings today offer a sad commentary on human nature. The prophet Jeremiah laments that people who could be living, "like a tree planted by the stream," choose rather to, "dwell in the parched places of the wilderness." In the gospel reading from Luke, Jesus underscores this by proposing that some people are so resistant to change that even someone coming back from the dead wouldn't impress them. Most of us are not only comfortable with our habits and routines, we have certain ways of thinking and acting that we are obstinate about, even when those ways may be slowly killing us, driving good people out of our lives, or excluding us from a better quality life. "Nobody's going to tell me any different." "My mind is made up." "I haven't got a problem, you do!" All of us have our mind-sets or blind spots whose power comes from their usefulness in protecting an insecure ego. We construct walls around our vulnerable little worlds and defend them with everything we have. Rather than face a problem, for example, we put up a barrier to hide it. Our efforts, however, create only an illusion of security; denying a problem doesn't make it go away. What is unfortunate about all this construction work is that the defenses we put up not only fail to keep danger out, they keep us confined and imprisoned.

Jesus calls us to conversion and growth. This call comes with a promise for more enriched and happy living. He tells us, "I have come that you might have life, and life in abundance." We cannot have more abundant life, however, as long as we are unwilling to *change* whatever it is that prevents us from having it. The biggest handicap to a happier life is not lack of opportunity, but our lack of openness to change. We may know people, for example, who remain stuck in their misery, or deadly addictions, because they simply refuse to listen to reason. We need to examine, therefore, where we miss golden opportunities for advancement in life because of our self-imposed blindness.

What are your blind spots? What issues, criticisms or suggestions are you most resistant about? Accept that defensiveness is generally an excellent clue of what you need to change most. Take a chance and lower your defenses. Be open to consider what changes you might need to make. What are other people encouraging you to do? You are only human, so admit that you could be wrong in some position you take. If you want to improve the quality of your life, be willing at least to take down some prison walls.

MAKING THE MOST OF MISFORTUNE

"The very stone which the builders rejected has become the head of the corner." Jesus makes this statement about himself in today's gospel reading from Matthew and presents us with an important lesson for effective living. Most of us become disheartened by our misfortunes. We feel victimized and hopeless when difficulties multiply, and we lose motivation to deal with the problems at hand. Jesus encourages us, however, to look at misfortune from a more positive perspective. What the Lord tells us is that every misfortune we endure has a redeeming value. Upsets can be used to advantage, and problems, however painful, can be made productive. Stones can be tossed at us, but we can use them as building material to make a better life for ourselves. The trick is maintaining a positive attitude.

All of us face setbacks and disappointments in different ways. Some people go down in defeat with their misfortunes, while others use their setbacks as important learning experiences. Problems, therefore, are not the problem; the way we handle them is. One married couple, for example, sees hopelessness in their differences of opinion and ends up in divorce court, while another sees "variety" in their differences and finds enrichment in their relationship. We need to recognize that every problem we face has a purpose for us or else it wouldn't be *our* problem. We are never afflicted with more than we can handle. God never lets a stone fall in our way if we don't have the ability to pick it up and make it into a cornerstone. There are no such things in life, therefore, as unredeemable mistakes, defeats, or failures, only *results* that we need to work on to further our development and happiness.

Jesus rose in glory on Easter, but he first had to go through the infamy of Good Friday. Can you accept that Easters are generally preceded by Good Fridays? If so, consider any problem, setback, or misfortune you might currently be facing. Take a moment to look at it for some positive value it might hold for you. What lesson is your pain trying to teach you? Search for an answer rather than stewing in depression. Where is the silver lining in the cloud? Work for resolutions instead of lamenting on how such things could be happening to you. Turn stones into cornerstones by focusing on redemptive possibilities. Rather than complaining, "Why me?", begin asking, "How can this serve me?"

SATURDAY OF THE SECOND WEEK OF LENT
Micah 7:14–15, 18–20   Luke 15:1–3, 11–32

PEOPLE PROBLEMS

Most of our problems in life are people problems. We are never more upset than when our relationships go sour or when people we count on disappoint us. If we feel we are taken for granted, or that our efforts are not appreciated, we can become irritated to no end. There are people who have irritated us enough that we can hold grudges against them for a lifetime. This leads us to a beautiful story told by Jesus and recorded in the gospel reading from Luke—the parable of the prodigal son. A young man runs off and squanders his inheritance in loose living. When he loses everything and comes back to his senses, he returns home to his father who welcomes him with open arms and not a word of recrimination. Jesus used this story to indicate God's acceptance, tolerance, and compassion for us whenever we stray from our values and make mistakes. Jesus also used this story to indicate that this should be our attitude in the way we treat one another.

It's worth considering how much our life would change if we could embrace God's compassionate attitude toward our fellow human beings. Think how much irritation and anger would be eliminated from our day-to-day living. Consider how much our serenity, peace, and joy would increase if we could accept the weaknesses of human nature, the ease with which we all make mistakes, and how important it is to have a forgiving heart. It's true that most of our problems are people problems, but those problems are there, for the most part, because we set ourselves up with unrealistic, inflexible, and unloving attitudes. People don't disappoint us as much as *we* become disappointed because *our* expectations are not met. If we could relax a little more and accept people as they are, warts and all, most of our problems would decrease significantly.

The reading from the prophet Micah shows God's chosen people receiving hope of deliverance because God understands their hearts and is willing to forgive their transgressions. Try to understand the human heart yourself. Think of how easy it is for you to make mistakes, and how hopeful you are that other people will be understanding. Can you return this favor to others? Can you see everyone, no matter what they do, with eyes of tolerance and compassion? Frustration and disappointment will disappear from your life the more you accept people as they are, with their own weaknesses and failings. Can you understand?

MONDAY OF THE THIRD WEEK OF LENT
2 Kings 5:1–15a Luke 4:24–30

A SIMPLE WAY OUT

Most of us complain about how busy we are, how stressed out we feel and how complicated life has become. With all the advances in technology, we had anticipated that life would run smoother. Such is not the case, however, because every "advance" seems to bring its own complications. Computers, for example, do in moments what once took hours and days, but the instruction manuals that accompany computer programs are often as thick as a phone book and can take months to master. Many of us may long, therefore, for a less complicated life. The good news is that a simple and less stressful way of living is within reach, and the readings today offer some suggestions.

Things don't have to be complicated if we don't want them to be. In the reading from Kings, for example, the military man, Naamen, is stricken with leprosy and comes to the prophet Elisha for a cure. Elisha bids him to go bathe in a local river. As a commander of the Syrian army, however, Naamen is a very complicated man and goes into "a rage" over such a simplistic and untoward approach to a cure. But, in the end, a dip in the river is all it takes.

Life is not complicated; *we* complicate life with our own inventiveness. We have substantial maintenance problems, for instance, because we own so much. We buy "time and labor saving" gadgets and find that they take even more time and labor to use and clean. We have enormous expectations of people and end up with enormous disappointments. It is possible, however, to bring a great measure of peace and simplicity to our lives if we turn some of our attitudes and actually look for simple solutions and remedies. In the gospel reading from Luke, we see an example of Jesus in handling difficult people and dangerous situations—he simply walks away.

Uncomplicate your life with a quest for simplicity. Tell the truth, and you won't have to work at cover-up stories. If your job is really more than you can take, quit and find an easier one. Avoid unhealthy habits and it is likely your health will take care of itself. If bad news wearies you, turn off the television. Stop believing every commercial and you won't be so depressed that you're missing something important. Stop worrying about what the neighbors think and you won't have to do so much to make good impressions. Change your priorities and you may find you don't have to be so busy. Always keep in mind the part you play in making life complicated. A simple way out may be just a matter of walking away.

TUESDAY OF THE THIRD WEEK OF LENT
Daniel 3:2, 11–20 **Matthew 18:21–35**

HARDLY WORTH THE PRICE

We might well agree that life would be unbearable if we human beings weren't forgiving of one another. We all have our faults and we hurt one another, even those we might love dearly; intentionally, and unintentionally, we do it again and again. Without forgiveness, life would be an endless series of vendettas and reprisals. We need to receive forgiveness, therefore, and we need to forgive. At the same time, however, we might not agree with the apparently extreme position Jesus takes on forgiveness that we observe in the reading from Matthew. Jesus tells Peter that we should forgive "seventy times seven times." What Jesus means is that we should forgive and forgive, and never stop forgiving. Doesn't this seem unreasonable, however? After all, "I have my limits," "there is only so much I can take," and, "I can handle strike one, even strike two, but strike three, and you're out!"

In our justice system, repeat offenders get maximum sentences. In our private justice systems, we may be willing to give someone who offends us a break, but then we tend to hold the line. What Jesus is promoting, however, is that we don't maintain *any* line. What Jesus encourages is that we develop forgiveness as a permanent frame of mind—not forgiving this or that, or this many times, but forgiveness as a blanket policy, with no restrictions whatever. And he encourages this for good reason. There is something damaging about any lack of forgiveness— damaging not to the perpetrator of an offense, but to anyone holding onto a grievance. At the end of this gospel passage, Jesus speaks about a forgiving king handing over an unforgiving servant to the jailers. What Jesus clearly suggests is that we put *ourselves* into prison with lack of forgiveness and demands for retribution.

Who really gets hurt when you are full of anger, resentfulness and a clamoring need for self-satisfaction? Is it the person you resent or despise? How much do you punish yourself by lack of forgiveness? Search your soul for anyone against whom you hold a grievance, and for your own well-being, let it go. Let forgiveness become your general policy for any and all offenses against you—no matter who; no matter for what; no matter how often. For Jesus, forgiveness is an act of self-liberation when it is practiced as a way of life. And while forgiveness may be difficult at times, it is hardly worth the price you pay by having your "limits."

WEDNESDAY OF THE THIRD WEEK OF LENT
Deuteronomy 4:1, 5–9 **Matthew 5:17–19**

LAW OR LOVE?

Often in the gospels we encounter Jesus in dispute with the scribes and Pharisees over the law and how it should be kept. We observe the Pharisees demanding literal observance of the law, while Jesus speaks of love as superior to the law. As a consequence, Jesus is considered a law breaker and religious anarchist. This had much to do with why the scribes and Pharisees sought his downfall. In the reading from Matthew, however, we hear Jesus speak strongly in favor of the law's observance, right down to its minute details. Are we reading a contradiction here? The contradiction, however, is only apparent; there is no opposition between love and the law. We can't be loving without keeping just laws. Loving people just might be the most law-abiding citizens we can find. A loving person, for example, will not endanger the lives of others with reckless driving or the misuse of firearms. All good laws are meant for our well-being and protection. But love also has the well-being of others at heart. Where love differs from law is that it prompts us to do what the law requires, and more, without having to be told.

When Jesus speaks of the law's observance, down to the "iota," he implies that love too should be observed in specific details. Someone in love, for example, is sensitive to whatever might affect a loved one's happiness. Love is proven in behavior, not just in romantic words or tender feelings. Most of us think of ourselves as generally loving. But this evaluation is subject to question if our routine actions do not consistently demonstrate love. We can believe all we want that we are loving, but if our behavior, down to the small details, does not mirror this belief, we're not being authentic. For Jesus, love is what love *does*.

What does your behavior say about your lovingness? How do your actions speak for your heart? Let the law remind you that love too needs to be demonstrated in concrete ways. Express your love in the ordinary details of daily life. A smile, a kind word, a little favor, an intimate joke, sharing an experience, holding back criticism, a compliment, giving in over a trivial argument, a midday call to someone you care about—all this is love in action. Jesus is not contradicting himself in speaking about the importance of love and the law. If you really are a loving person, you will show your love in a thousand direct and indirect ways. Love like this covers every "iota" of the law.

THURSDAY OF THE THIRD WEEK OF LENT
Jeremiah 7:23–28 **Luke 11:14–23**

PERSONS OF INTEGRITY

It's not uncommon to hear people remark that, "everything's falling apart today." There is a general feeling among many of us that the world is coming apart at the seams. There is little common spirit that pulls us together as a society. Values aren't what they used to be. Political, even spiritual, leaders have lost the trust and respect they once commanded. Millions claim they don't know what to believe in anymore. Furthermore, this feeling of disintegration is also reflected in us as individuals. It is not uncommon, for example, to hear people comment that they are becoming "unglued." When we talk this way, what we are saying is that we have lost a sense of integrity; we are missing something that ties our life together. And there are clear reasons why this is so. Maybe we've grown comfortable living with double standards. There are parents, for example, who warn their teenagers about smoking and drinking while doing nothing to disabuse themselves of these habits. We may get angry over our children's argumentativeness and yet bicker bitterly with our spouse. We may be so concerned with impressing other people that we never express what we really think or feel until it gets to the point where we don't know anymore what we really think or feel. Maybe we try to do too much, or too many things at the same time, with the result that our work suffers, our family life suffers, and we suffer. Perhaps we place value on our Christian beliefs and also on secular beliefs that totally contradict them. It's impossible to live a double life without paying the penalty.

In the reading from Luke, Jesus warns that "Every kingdom divided against itself is laid waste, and house falls upon house." When we are divided in ourselves, we're guaranteed stressful living and ultimate breakdown. What Jesus encourages is that we be persons of integrity. If we don't want to feel "unglued," we need to work at pulling ourselves together. The antidote to "falling apart" is a conscious pursuit of an integrated life. Living strictly by our Christian values is one of the best ways to achieve it.

"Glue" yourself together by eliminating double standards and living fully as a Christian. Establish your priorities and values, and stick by them. What should be important in your life, and what isn't worth the time and effort in the long run? Nothing can better help build your integrity than a commitment to truth. Say what you mean, and mean what you say.

THE MOST FORGOTTEN COMMANDMENT

Lent is a "penitential" season, a time we reflect on our sinfulness and seek God's forgiveness. In evaluating our sins we most often use the Commandments as a guideline. We repent that we have cheated, hurt someone's feelings, entertained malicious thoughts; been covetous, proud, and deceitful. Most of us, however, neglect to consider the most important commandment of all. In the gospel reading from Mark, Jesus affirms that the greatest commandment is: "... you shall love the Lord your God with all your heart, and with all your soul, and with all your mind, and with all your strength." When we confess our sins, this commandment is likely the most forgotten. And the reason is not difficult to understand. It is easy to become sidetracked from giving attention to what really matters in life. We can become so preoccupied with insignificant details that we fail to see what's going on in the big picture. We can labor, for example, at building a dream home for our family without noticing that our family is falling apart. We can work ourselves to the bone to provide "the good life" and never find time to sit back and enjoy it. We may even be so dedicated to Christian activities that we neglect our relationship with God.

To keep ourselves in perspective, it is imperative that we be concerned about our relationship with God, first and foremost. Jesus clearly affirms that our relationship with God must be our most important concern. Loving God wholeheartedly keeps us in focus and pulls our life together in an integrated way. Somehow, if our relationship with God is right, everything else in our life seems to fall into place.

How do you view your relationship with God? How often do you consider how well you are obeying the commandment that is "first of all"? Is prayer as important to you as performing good deeds? Do you feel comfortable speaking to God about your life and its needs? God wishes to live with you on an intimate basis that can only be spoken about in terms of love. Make love of God a priority in your life. Love of God is no different from any other loving relationship you enjoy. Speak to God as a friend and helpmate. Talk to God about your concerns and worries. Tell God what a delight it is to have the pleasure of the Spirit's company, and always be grateful for how much God loves you. Ask the Spirit to help you love God above all things in this world. God will answer your prayer and show you how.

SATURDAY OF THE THIRD WEEK OF LENT
Hosea 5:15c–6:6 Luke 18:9–14

WAKE-UP CALL

In fairy tales, the handsome prince and beautiful maiden overcome a set of obstacles and then go off to their castle to live happily ever after. In real life, however, we know this is rarely the case. Honeymoons come to an end. We may ride high for weeks but eventually moods change. We may enjoy months of uninterrupted good health but sooner or later we become ill. Fortune may smile on us for years and then some terrible misfortune strikes. Bad things do happen to good people. When they do, we are devastated: "how could God let this happen?"; "why is God doing this to me?" Our perplexity is understandable. After all, if we try to lead a good life, why should we have to suffer? We often fail to take into account, however, something important about pain, setbacks, misfortunes, and suffering. When everything is going our way, we tend to settle in and get comfortable. When things go smoothly in our life, we become content with routine and apathetic about challenging ourselves. In short, we come to a standstill in our personal development. Normally, something has to come along to get us moving again; something has to wake us from our slumber and shake us from our complacency.

People usually don't give up bad habits unless a crisis intervenes. Marriages and friendships don't develop to new levels of relationship without facing problems. We normally won't consider developing new talents and skills unless we lose our employment. It often isn't until we get sick that we consider better ways of taking care of our health. Our spiritual life usually doesn't advance unless our old beliefs are shaken. In the reading from the prophet Hosea, we hear that God, "has torn, that he may heal us; he has stricken, and he will bind us up." God knows when we are ready to move on, and ahead, in our life. What we learn from Hosea is that God uses disruptions and suffering as a wake-up call to prompt us onward toward our destiny. We are not meant to "settle down," but to develop our unlimited potential. Whatever we suffer, God is encouraging us to grow.

Can you see your afflictions from a more positive point of view? Have you not learned important lessons from the hardships you've endured in the past? Are you aware, perhaps, of how passive and apathetic you get when things come too easy for you? There is much truth in, "no pain, no gain." "How can God let this happen to me?" Because God loves you and is concerned about your growth and development.

MONDAY OF THE FOURTH WEEK OF LENT
Isaiah 65:17–21 **John 4:43–54**

FAITH WORKS MIRACLES

Faith is certainly important to us as Christians, but we may not appreciate the dynamics of faith as a means of enhancing our life. We may know what a belief *is*, but not be aware of what believing *does*. There are many things we accept on faith, but we normally don't see faith as a power to live more effectively. We may even think faith has little to do with practical living. Many people believe faith has its place in their lives, but don't use it to produce a better quality life for themselves and others. In the gospel reading from John, however, we witness something important about the true nature of faith. An official implores Jesus to come and cure his son who is at the point of death. Jesus simply tells the man to go back home and that his son will live. The man believes, and the son lives. What we need to recognize is not only that Jesus worked a miracle, but so did the official's believing.

Beliefs as such are static. Faith on the other hand works miracles; there is nothing static about it at all. How is this so? Faith is not an abstract set of beliefs but an *energy* that sets things in motion. When we believe in other people, for example, we bring out the best in them. Good teachers and counselors know this about their students and clients. Students can be *believed* into greater academic achievement; clients can be believed into better mental and emotional health. Doctors can help patients believe themselves into healing. When spouses believe in each other, and parents believe in their children, wonderful things begin to happen. Faith makes things happen. When we believe in ourselves, we become enthusiastic; it's belief we have in our dreams that makes them come true.

Whether you believe you "can," or you "can't," you're right, because faith is self-fulfilling. Never discount the power of faith. Faith will work for you or against you, so use it to your advantage. What you believe about yourself will turn you into exactly the person you believe in. The same applies to what you believe about others as well. Experiment with the power of believing. What, for example, do you need to give yourself a better quality life? Believe with all your heart that you can attain it. Let faith keep you unshakeably focused on your objective. Remain faith-full and you will fulfill your dreams. Also, use faith to bring out the best in others. Believe in them, and watch miracles happen.

RISE, AND WALK

The gospel reading from John contains an important lesson in self-responsibility. The narrative concerns a miracle Jesus performs for an invalid, and a further dispute about breaking the Sabbath law, but there is a story within a story here. The invalid has spent many long years at the side of the pool of Bethzatha, waiting for someone to immerse him in its miraculous waters. He remains unhealed because no one comes to his assistance. The man merits a cure through Jesus, however, not by having Jesus lower him into the pool, but by obeying Jesus' command to "rise, and walk." The lesson here is revealing. Most of us never get what we want out of life because we basically sit around waiting and hoping for it to happen. We don't achieve the happiness we desire because we expect someone else to provide it for us. We are sincere in our desires, even passionate in our hopes, but we confuse sincerity and passion with the need for personal effort.

As small children we became accustomed to being cared for and the expectation never quite leaves us. We may love to have other people do things for us. We may want others to solve our problems, carry the blame for our mistakes, bear all the responsibility for a relationship, and make us feel better when we are hurting. Perhaps we figure that, if we wait or complain long enough, or look pitiful enough, someone will eventually come to our assistance. This isn't the way life is meant to be, however. In our personal evolution, it is expected that we grow up, begin doing things for ourselves, and become self-sufficient. We are not meant to be dependent children forever. This doesn't mean that we can't depend on other people to be helpful, but that we primarily take full responsibility for ourselves. In the gospel reading, Jesus admonishes the former invalid: "See, you are well! Sin no more, that nothing worse befall you." What Jesus is encouraging is that the man learn a lesson from getting up and walking, and not go back to waiting upon others to do what he needs to do for himself.

How dependent do you *make* yourself on others? Do what you need to do to take care of yourself. Ask for help when you need it, but never at the expense of turning over to others the responsibility for your well-being and happiness. Watch how your self-esteem increases the more you do for yourself. Take the initiative to go after what you think is important. If you wait for success and happiness to happen, you may wait a lifetime. Rise, and walk.

WEDNESDAY OF THE FOURTH WEEK OF LENT
Isaiah 49:8–15 John 5:17–30

"I WILL NOT FORGET YOU"

One of the worst feelings we can experience as human beings is abandonment. The feeling is even more acute when we suffer alone or without the support of caring people. While it is important that we be self-sufficient and independent, it is also important that we find the support we need to face our challenges and problems. By nature, we are social creatures; we are not meant to go it alone. The reading from the prophet Isaiah is eloquent in its assurance of God's unrelenting support for us: "Can a woman forget her sucking child, that she should have no compassion on the son of her womb? Even these may forget, yet I will not forget you." Are any words more beautiful to the ear, especially when we find ourselves burdened with sorrow and affliction? These words should warm our hearts and fortify our resolutions. If we can appreciate that God is always with us, and always behind us, we should be able to handle whatever we may have to face in life.

But, we might object, while the thought that God supports us is certainly pious, it doesn't do much to actually console us in moments of need. It's wonderful to know that God believes in us and loves us, but God seems so distant. God's support isn't something we can *feel*. This objection, therefore, turns our attention to the importance of having an ongoing personal relationship with God. There can be people in our lives who would be full of understanding, compassion and love for us, but we have to build up a relationship with them. It is up to us to communicate, express our needs, and be grateful for a listening ear. Do we think it will be any different in our relationship with God? We need to come to terms with what we really believe about God's presence in us. It is necessary for us to actively reach out to God, person to person, and talk to God about our needs for help.

> Be real in your relationship with God; relate to God as a real person. The more deeply prayerful you become, the more you will feel God's presence and care. But you must do your part to reach out. Compose yourself in silence more often and, above all, learn to listen to what God may have to say. It is God's good pleasure to help you in all your needs, and God will speak to you. This help may come as a sudden impulse, an inspiration, a sudden release of anxiety, a burst of energy, a surprise happening, or someone saying just the right thing at just the right moment. "I will not forget you," is God's solemn pledge. Take advantage of it.

THURSDAY OF THE FOURTH WEEK OF LENT
Exodus 32:7–14 **John 5:31–47**

PROOF IN THE DEED

In the gospel reading from John, Jesus defends himself against those who disbelieve in him by pointing to his deeds as proof that he is doing God's work: "these very works which I am doing bear witness that the Father has sent me." We should be able to relate to this. Most of us would agree that "actions speak louder than words." People can talk a good game, but it is their actions that tell us most about their character and believability. Everyone claims to have good intentions, and everyone says they want to do the right thing, but what kinds of actions follow all these assurances of sincerity? No one loses credibility faster, for example, than someone who pleads trustworthiness and then talks behind our back at the first opportunity.

We need to examine our own credibility, however. We may feel righteous in our pursuit of a decent life, and consider ourselves loving persons. We may feel strongly about the value of the Christian way of life and believe ourselves to be good Christians. We may even feel set apart from the more godless, immoral, or material-minded people among whom we live and work. But what do our actions prove? How, for example, are we "set apart" as Christians? Practically speaking, where do we differ from people who don't share the Christian beliefs we hold sacred? Do we behave any differently from friends and neighbors who may have no religious beliefs at all? Do we face life and our problems with more hope and confidence than an atheist? Are we more generous, compassionate, and forgiving than a fellow worker who has never crossed the door of a church in his or her life? What makes us stand out as Christians? What do we *do* that makes us credible?

"What you see is what you get." Could this be said about you? Does your behavior generally reflect what you say you believe and value? What proof do you offer that you do have good intentions and that you want to do the right thing? Actions give witness to what you are more than fine words and impressive credentials. *Be* a good Christian, not only in what you believe but in what you do. Speak the truth, even when it is difficult. Look for good even in people you find obnoxious. Be forgiving even when it seems you have every reason to bear a grudge. Offer your assistance even when it is likely your help will not be appreciated. Good intentions are certainly important, but the proof of what you are is in the deed.

WHEN TRUTH HURTS

The reading from the book of Wisdom points out a sad feature about human nature. Extraordinary people may sometimes win our admiration, but it's just as likely they get on our nerves. Wisdom says: "He became to us a reproof of our thoughts; the very sight of him is a burden to us, because his manner of life is unlike that of others, and his ways are strange." The productivity of others can make us ashamed of our lack of achievement. In the light of other people's goodness, our faults can stand out in bold relief. In view of their successes, our failings can appear reprehensible. Such is the case of Jesus, in the reading from the gospel of John. We can only wonder why it could be said about Jesus, "Is not this the man whom they seek to kill?" It is obvious that the good works Jesus performs, and the message of love he preaches, win him as many enemies as friends. When he issues a call for repentance, he stings the hearts of those who hear it. Truth often hurts. Many people don't want to hear the truth about themselves. We like to believe we are good enough as we are, as loving as we can be, and that our hearts are in the right place. When something someone does calls this into question, we respond with resentment rather than interest.

If we are sincere about our growth and development, however, we may need a big change in attitude. If others are succeeding where we are not, we should use them as models, rather than objects of resentment. For our own sake, if we desire a better and happier life for ourselves we need to be open to suggestion, criticism, and challenge. It's a fact that other people may know us better than we know ourselves; other people may be more honest with us than we are with ourselves. Even enemies can sometimes be good friends because of a truth they reveal about us.

Do extraordinary people irritate you, or motivate you? Are you inclined to see the goodness and success of others as a as a reproof to yourself, or as an example of what you might achieve? How do you handle criticism, or even unsolicited advice? Remember that truth hurts only when it *is* the truth. Be committed to truth, especially when it hurts, because a valuable lesson is being offered to you. Everyone needs improvement and everyone can profit from the input of others. Weigh all criticism for its merits. Be grateful for any input that can help you build a better quality life.

SATURDAY OF THE FOURTH WEEK OF LENT
Jeremiah 11:18–20 **John 7:40–53**

OUT OF THE MOUTHS OF BABES

The gospel reading from John offers a lesson that truth is the truth, no matter who or what may be its source. The narrative presents a dispute over where Jesus gets the authority to speak the way he does. Many are impressed with the message and challenge that Jesus delivers; others are looking for ways to discredit it. The ruse his dis-creditors use is an old one: if you don't like what someone is saying, attack the character of the one saying it. "Search," they say, "and you will find that no prophet is to rise from Galilee." We're not disinclined, of course, to do this ourselves. When someone chastises us, or calls something we do into question, we usually go immediately on the defensive. "What do you know?" "Look who's talking!" "Since when are you an authority?" When we don't want to hear something about ourselves, our best defense is an offense; we try to discredit anyone putting our faults into the limelight. When a spouse, for example, observes how crabby or unappreciative we've become, we may retort: "You're one to talk!"

Sometimes what we need to hear most about ourselves comes from the most unauthorized sources. People we work with on a daily basis, for example, may be able to tell more about our state of health, our emotional stability, our ability to get things done, and our moral character than a doctor, psychologist, boss, or clergyman. Children often have a keenness of observation that we generally don't give them credit for. When a son or a daughter reproaches us for not telling the full truth, it can sting us. But, "out of the mouths of babes," truth is truth whatever its origin. One does not need to be an "expert" to be wise, nor does someone need to be "licensed" to be right on target in evaluating our behavior. It is to our own well-being and happiness that we learn to consider the truth from wherever it comes.

Are you willing to consider a truth about yourself, no matter its source? Do you automatically discount the insights of others just because they disturb you? Serve your own best interests by an openness to learn from everybody, without a demand for "credentials." You can change and build a better quality life for yourself often by simply listening to your own family members and people with whom you work. Muster the courage and humility to go off the defensive. You have nothing to fear from the truth, and everything to gain.

MONDAY OF THE FIFTH WEEK OF LENT
Daniel 13:1–9, 15–17, 19–30, 33–62 **John 8:1–11**

THE LAST TO THROW STONES

It is strange about human nature that we feel shame over our failings and fight to keep them hidden, yet we revel in exposing those of others. We hate being judged and evaluated by superiors and peers and yet often have little hesitation about judging other people. We're resentful when someone tries to change us to fit their expectations, and yet may have no reluctance to try to change someone else to fit ours. A touching and instructive lesson in this respect is given to us in the gospel reading from John. A woman has been caught in adultery and is paraded before a crowd that gets ready to stone her to death. The scribes and Pharisees pursue Jesus for comment, hoping "to test him."

Jesus simply offers a challenge: "Let him who is without sin among you be the first to throw a stone at her." With the possibility of their own sins being exposed, they "went away, one by one, beginning with the eldest."

The lesson is not so much about the compassion of Jesus, but about his implication that we get out of the habit of judging and condemning anyone. The reading clearly suggests that people who are most willing to throw stones at others are usually the least justified in doing so. Furthermore, while it is unavoidable that we make judgments about people we need to avoid, about people we should hire or dismiss, or about people we might like to befriend or marry, we run into serious problems when we are *judgmental*. How often are we completely accurate in our evaluations of others, even those we love dearly? We rarely know the motives behind what other people do, so how much truth do we think we attain? Furthermore, being judgmental makes us suspicious of everyone's motives and can prevent us from enjoying potentially rewarding relationships. And, even more damaging to ourselves, judging others basically distracts us from giving appropriate attention to our own faults and problems. If we are constantly evaluating others, we waste time and energy that could better serve the purposes of our own growth.

How judgmental are you? Do you find yourself more than ready to criticize others? Do you perhaps deflect from looking at your own faults by pointing out those of others? Take note of how much judging of others you do in a given day. Consider how grateful you should be that your own faults are not up for constant inspection. Work on yourself and let others be. The older you get, the quicker you should be willing to walk away.

PRESENT LIVING

In the reading from Numbers, Moses has his hands full with the complaints of God's chosen people. They suffered untold humiliation, injustice, and persecution in the land of Egypt and then, instead of enjoying their freedom and the journey to the promised land, they complained about the food, and wanted to return to their former misery. They weren't happy where they were in Egypt; they weren't happy where they were in the desert; they didn't seem too happy about where they were going. The plague of the fiery serpents was little more than a reflection of their own chronic dissatisfactions.

There is a lesson here of great importance for effective living. If we can't learn to be happy in the present moment, we will never be happy at all. If we can't appreciate the good we have, right now, we will never have it good. It is up to us to decide in what time frame we wish to live. Many people choose to live in the past. They are forever looking backward and talking about how good things used to be. They may talk about events in high school or college as if nothing better has happened since. Some reach middle age and are convinced that the best days of their lives are over. Others, on the other hand, live in the future. They will be happy "if only," and "when. . .." If only they could get a better job, or move to the suburbs, or have more friends, or get over this misfortune, they would find contentment. Or, when they get married, or divorced, or win the lottery, or retire, everything will start coming up roses. The problem, of course, is that neither the past nor the future exists; all there is, is NOW. It's important that we plan for the future, it's important that we remember the lessons of the past, but living in the present is most important of all. This means focusing on NOW, and appreciating everything we have at present.

In what time zone do you spend the major part of your day? Can you appreciate the futility of living in the past or the future? Find happiness in who you are, and what you have, in the present. Be grateful for the many blessings that come into your life every day. This doesn't mean you forget what you've gained through experience, or that you stop setting goals for your improvement, only that you relish where you are at the present moment. Focus on the relationships you currently enjoy, your good health, the gifts of the season. Accept right now as where you are meant to be. Embrace even your problems as belonging to you, right now, for a reason. Everything you need to be happy, you have NOW.

WEDNESDAY OF THE FIFTH WEEK OF LENT
Daniel 3:14–20, 91–92, 95 John 8:31–42

THE TRUTH WILL MAKE YOU FREE

One of the most quoted statements of Jesus regularly appears on religious billboards, on the logo of many educational institutions, in banners gracing the waiting rooms of psychotherapists, and in the speeches of politicians: "The truth will make you free." Since we all hunger for freedom, we might do well to ponder this expression in the gospel reading, and consider *how* truth frees us. In the first place, we might examine how falsehood takes away our freedom. We may have misguided beliefs about what it takes to make us happy, and they prevent us from finding true ways of making a better life for ourselves. Lying, cheating, and other forms of deceit corrode the self-respect that is essential to freedom. As Jesus states in the gospel reading: "Truly, truly, I say to you, everyone who commits sin is a slave to sin." We are never more "slaves" than when we are hooked on sinful ways. We may even forfeit freedom to grow and enjoy a more enriched life by maintaining illusions that we have "arrived," or that we have little more to learn, or that our development has gone about as far as it can.

Truth, on the other hand, makes us free because it allows us to see ourselves as we really are, and to evaluate what is really important in life. Truth frees us from our illusions, our need to put on false fronts to impress other people, and our compulsiveness to see things only our way. Truth puts us at ease with ourselves, builds our sense of humor, and frees us from taking ourselves and our problems too seriously. The love of truth humbles us and gives us the freedom to be open to suggestions and criticism from others, without going immediately on the defensive. Finally, the example of Shadrach, Meshach, and Abednego, in the reading from Daniel, demonstrates that we can be free from harm in any "fiery furnace," if we live by honest values and refuse to compromise our integrity.

Jesus invites you to follow him as the Way, the Truth, and the Life. Love of truth is one of the best ways to follow in the Lord's footsteps. Consider how many problems, and how much suffering, you bring into your life with false beliefs about yourself, unrealistic expectations of others, and pursuits of illusions and fantasy. Enjoy the freedom only truth can bring. Refuse to live a life-style that compromises your values. Commit yourself to honesty and truthfulness in everything you do. Freedom is as close as a simple decision for truth above all things. Any truth frees you from something.

THURSDAY OF THE FIFTH WEEK OF LENT
Genesis 17:3–9 John 8:51–59

GOD'S COVENANT WITH US

The reading from Genesis describes a covenant God made with Abraham. God chose Abraham for great things. He was to be "fruitful," and the father of a "multitude of nations." With the covenant, God promised Abraham and all his descendants unremitting support in fulfilling their destiny. It would be unfortunate, however, if we miss the point of how this promise applies to us. We often fail to appreciate that God has also sworn a covenant with us, personally. From the day of birth, we too are chosen for greatness. We exist because, out of all the infinite possibilities of those who could have been born, God willed us, specifically, to be. If God didn't so will it, we wouldn't be here. Each of us, therefore, has a purpose in God's design. We are expected to be "fruitful," and God promises unremitting support that we might fulfill our destiny.

New meaning and excitement come into our lives the minute we begin seeing ourselves from our Creator's perspective. Millions of people go through life with little more ambition than to survive without too many hassles. They never appreciate the part they play in a grand design and downplay any suggestion of more "fruitful" development. Perhaps seeing themselves as a little cog in a big machine, they never come to terms with their unrivaled uniqueness and purpose. Many come to the end of their lives only to discover they never "lived" at all. All of us have a tendency to sell ourselves short with, "I'm too old," or "I'm not educated," or "I'm not a strong person." We concentrate on our weakness rather than our possibilities and fear trying something new. This, however, is not appropriate thinking for a child of the "covenant." No matter how we try to hide from it, we have a destiny to be "fruitful." God is glorified as we grow in our talents and interests, in our openness and love, and in our pursuit of excellence.

Come to terms with the reason of your birth. You are made for greatness and God has made a covenant with you. Can you understand that your vivid imagination and the very dreams you have for a better life are part of God's promise to help you fulfill your destiny? Are you cynical about your possibilities? Let the reading from Genesis encourage you. Fill your life with enthusiasm by appreciating that you are "destined." Search out ways to expand your life. Multiply your friendships; read, study, travel, try something new. Come to the end of your days with an assurance that you have lived a "full" life. God will be in his glory, and so will you.

"You Are Gods"

In the gospel reading, we hear Jesus make an intriguing statement. He is being accused of blasphemy because, being a man, he makes himself out to be God. Jesus responds to this accusation with a quotation from Scripture: "you are gods." Jesus' contention is that, if this is so about the ordinary people being addressed, how can it be blasphemy for him to claim this prerogative to himself? You are gods! Is this a misuse of language in claiming this about human beings, or a fall back to paganism? How are we to understand its meaning and significance? We might begin by understanding something about Jesus as God's incarnation. For all his statements concerning an intimate relationship with his Father in heaven, Jesus never arrogated this relationship to himself alone. As a matter of fact, in the many teachings of Jesus, he so emphasized our intimate connection with God, that he revealed a clue as to our true identity. Jesus clearly taught that we share God's life and that God lives in us. Spirit is spirit, without time or divisions. We do not come into being apart from our Creator; as spiritual beings, we are part of God. Each of us is God's self-revelation, and incarnation, in this world.

Our purpose in life is to live our true identity and manifest God's glory. Our life is meant to reflect the life we have with God; everything we do is meant to reveal the divinity we share. In other words, we ought to *act* like gods. And there is nothing at all blasphemous about this. Scripture assures us that we are indeed "children of God." We should never hesitate to take this affirmation at its word. None of us is "low born," therefore, nor can any of us be described as coming from "bad stock." As children of God, the day should not go by that we don't take pride in our eternal heritage. Knowing who and what we really are can give us new confidence and motivation to become all we were created to be.

Because of the divine nature you share, you need never feel "insignificant," and nothing you do will be "unimportant." There is no greater lift for your self-confidence than knowing you are part of God, and there is no greater ambition you could aspire to than allowing God to shine through you. Life becomes "fulfilled" the more you reveal your divinity, and nothing will make you more attractive to others. What needs to be changed in your attitudes and behavior to reflect your belief that you are a child of God? What can you do in the way you think and act that will help reveal your true identity?

SATURDAY OF THE FIFTH WEEK OF LENT
Ezekiel 37:21–28 **John 11:45–57**

THE TEMPTATION OF EXPEDIENCY

The gospel reading offers us a study of human nature in a case of high drama. The Jewish authorities are gravely concerned over the numbers of followers Jesus is attracting because of the signs and wonders he performs. They fear that, if this phenomenon continues, "the Romans will come and destroy both our holy place and our nation." The high priest Caiaphas, however, is a practical man. He tells his compatriots: "You know nothing at all; you do not understand that it is expedient for you that one man should die for the people, and that the whole nation should not perish." Caiaphas embraced an expedient solution to the problem of Jesus. Rather than face Jesus, and examine the validity of his "signs," he prescribes taking the easy way out: kill Jesus and all problems will be solved.

Making tough decisions, always telling the truth, living up to our values, is often difficult. We human beings, therefore, have a tendency to take the easy way out. Why do it the hard way if there's an easy way? Why pay for something we might get for nothing? Why spend time examining the validity of someone's argument if we can drive him or her away with a put-down? Why work hard for success in business if we can get what we want quicker with a little cheating? We don't want anyone to get hurt, of course, but why not tell a little lie to get us out of trouble, or make up an excuse to get us out of an obligation, or feign illness to get someone else to do our job? Is it any wonder self-respect suffers in so many people with so much inauthentic living? And do we believe that expediency, rather than truth, is really the "easy" way out? We most often create even more problems for ourselves by looking for the expedient way out of our predicaments. One lie, for example, requires more lies. The death of Jesus didn't solve any national problems for the Jewish authorities.

Expediency is a great temptation to avoid accountability, but it always ends up costing more. Can you see it this way? Are you inclined to face your issues, no matter what, or do you look for the easy way out? Are you in the habit, for example, of blaming others rather than assuming responsibility for what happens in your life? Learn to muster more courage in making tough decisions and handling your predicaments. You will find that you have more than it takes to live authentically, and that living responsibly is generally the easiest way out.

Monday of Holy Week
Isaiah 42:1–7 **John 12:1–11**

Going All Out

Most of us find it particularly insulting to be considered "cheap." We may be frugal and conservative in our life-styles but we find it shameful to be thought of as stingy. Why is this so? Perhaps it's because we hope others will be unstinting and generous to us in our needs. Maybe it's because we know how respected generous people are, and would like to give the impression that we too share that respectability. The question is, however, why try to give impressions when we can live the real thing? Magnanimity, going all out, is basically a style of living that we can easily adopt. We have the option of living our lives continuously from a perspective of abundance. Generosity is a sign that we have come to appreciate that life is abundant in its gifts; that we grow rich in sharing rather than hoarding; that there is more joy in giving than receiving. In the gospel reading from John, we see Mary anointing Jesus with a very expensive ointment. And we note she is lavishly pouring it out on his feet. Doesn't this reveal something of this woman's loving nature? Are we not moved by her extravagance?

We don't have to be wealthy, however, or buy extravagant gifts, to demonstrate a generous nature, we can show it through our attitudes and behavior. We can go "all out," for example, in the way we approach our jobs, in the way we pay full attention to other people when they are talking to us, in the way we spend quality time with our friends, in the way we share whatever we already have. And ironically, the more generous we are of ourselves, the more we get back in return. Isn't it the friendliest people, for instance, who have the most friends, the most outgoing who experience the least loneliness?

Adopt abundance thinking as a rule of life. Live life from the wealth of its gifts rather than from fears that there isn't enough to go around. Find more ways you can share, rather than secure, what you own. Love always increases the more you give it away. Live to make other people happy and watch how much happiness comes into your own life. What you do for others, you end up doing for yourself. Practice bringing love, laughter, and joy into someone else's life. Share your wisdom and experience with the young; volunteer your time and skills in parish or community projects. Life is more alive the more you go all out to live it.

A MATTER OF LOYALTY

The suffering, death, and resurrection of Jesus are part of one of the greatest dramas of history. The passion of Jesus not only records his personal tragedy, it brings to light many tragic elements in the characters associated with him in this drama. The Jewish authorities, for example, plot the death of Jesus as a convenient means of getting rid of a potential rival. The cheering mob on Palm Sunday changes its mood to cries of "crucify him" on Good Friday. Pilate opts to send a man to his death for political expediency. Herod hopes to use Jesus for entertainment and expects to see him perform some marvelous tricks. The soldiers leisurely throw dice at the foot of the cross, callous to the horror of a crucifixion right above them. But perhaps the most heart-rending tragedy we observe in this drama is Jesus being betrayed by one of his own, and denied by the one who was "the rock upon whom I will build my church." We are moved by this betrayal and denial because perhaps we too may have been betrayed or denied by people we counted on most for loyalty and support. It is likely one of the worst disappointments we can endure.

What we should take from the gospel reading of John, therefore, is a lesson in loyalty. None of us should point a finger at Judas or Peter, without considering our own disloyalty. How often in a day do we betray our convictions for monetary gain, or our values for the sake of keeping up appearances? How often do we lie to save face? Perhaps there have been times we abandoned those who counted on our support. Have we lost friends because we weren't there for them in their moment of need? Are there members of our families who suffer because we shirk our responsibilities to them? The drama of the passion of Jesus is our drama. There are few characters in this story with whom we might not relate.

Loyalty is indispensable for living effectively. There is no respect like self-respect, and loyalty is one major way to sustain it. Spend some time today, therefore, reflecting on where you might be falling short on loyalty to someone who counts on you. Consider some of your major responsibilities to family and friends, and evaluate where you might be slacking off. Commit yourself to loyalty as a major principle by which you run your life. Ultimately, you will be judged not on your failings, but on your fidelity. Loyalty to the Lord, above all achievements, will have its reward.

WEDNESDAY OF HOLY WEEK
Isaiah 50:4–9a Matthew 26:14–25

FINAL VINDICATION

One common complaint we share at times is that nobody understands us or appreciates what we do. We make extraordinary efforts to do a job well but get no recognition. We put ourselves out to be helpful without receiving a word of thanks. Sometimes our actions are misunderstood; our good intentions are called into question, even by people who should know us better. Worse yet, there are times we are victims of injustice. People judge us on scraps of information and falsely condemn us. We might be an innocent bystander and stand accused of doing something wrong. An employer, for example, blames us for someone else's mistake. Where are we to find vindication?

The reading from the prophet Isaiah serves as a fitting conclusion to Lent. In the final analysis, it is futile to expect that justice will always be done in this world, and that people always get what they deserve, for good or for bad. The passion and death of Jesus is a good case in point. We live in a very imperfect world with very imperfect people who are very imperfect in the way they treat one another. We can never expect to be completely understood or appreciated; no one will ever totally comprehend our motives; we may often suffer unjustly, and without vindication. Isaiah encourages us, however, not to despair or feel shame, because, "he who vindicates me is near." Our only hope for vindication is God, who understands us completely and loves us unconditionally. But is this any consolation to us? Do we have to wait to meet God in heaven before justice is finally done? We need to listen to Isaiah more closely. He makes clear that our vindicator is "near." This encourages us to reflect on our personal relationship with God in *this* life. We can feel vindicated by God if we remain alert and appreciative of God's loving presence within us.

In prayer and meditation, continue to work on your personal relationship with God. God is "near" to you, closer than anyone else can be. Thank God for being present to you. Go to God with any need for vindication. If you are misunderstood and misjudged, allow God to be your vindicator. Stop expecting vindication from an imperfect world and imperfect people. God alone knows your heart and fully loves the goodness that is in you. When Jesus died on the cross, he committed himself to God alone: "Father, into your hands I commend my spirit." God was his final vindication, and ultimately, God is yours also.

POSTSCRIPT FOR EASTER

EXPERIENCE THE JOY
OF RESURRECTION

Easter joyfully concludes our journey through Lent, but, at the same time, offers us a challenge. We have made a pilgrimage of personal growth from ashes to Easter but our pilgrimage is far from over. As a matter of fact, it is never completed, because our potential for change and growth remains unlimited. Just as the first Easter spelled a beginning for the church, our celebration of Easter spells a beginning of the rest of our lives. Easter is but a temporary stop for us to reflect on the gains we have made in living more effectively, and to rejoice in those gains.

And it is important that we do rejoice. All of us can relate to Jesus in his Good Friday experience—we likely have had many of them over a lifetime. But we also need to relate to Jesus in his resurrection. We do this by taking just pride in our efforts to improve the quality of our lives and the lives of other people. We should have no hesitation in rewarding ourselves for our achievements. If our lenten journey has made us more understanding of our relationship to God, more appreciative of our calling as Christians, more compassionate, forgiving, and loving—we have come a long way. We need to sing and dance in delight over our accomplishments. This isn't arrogance or vanity but something we human beings need to keep us going. "Success breeds success." We become motivated to go on by the joy of knowing how far we have come.

Celebrate the little resurrections that go on in your life. Treat yourself to a pat on the back, a party, a special gift, a well-earned vacation, and the like. When you overcome a bad habit, widen your horizons with more education, improve your chances for more enhanced living, develop new talents, or grow in your love for others, rejoice. God delights in your successes to become more of what you are meant to be. God takes joy in your joy. Allow God the pleasure of seeing you happy in the experience of your resurrection in whatever form it appears.